THE HEALING MANUAL

A guide to healing.
How to experience health &
well-being in all areas of life.

By Tara Antler
BHSc, Intuitive, Love-Igniter,
Flourishing Life Coach &
Mentor, Reiki Master

Founder of Tara Healing Sanctuary;

The Heart of Flourishing;

The LIGHT Academy.

Beautiful Jenny!
You are such a BRIGHT LIGHT in this world! Wrapping you in joy, creativity & tons of expansion! Keep shining!
BIG hugs,
Tara

i

Living Vibrancy Training Institute
c/o Tara Antler
Hwy 17
Deux Rivieres, Ontario, K0J 1R0
www.livingvibrancy.com
tara@tarahealingsanctuary.com

To order additional books or to buy in bulk, please contact Living Vibrancy Training Institute at 647-991-9366.

To request author information, or for speaker or other media requests, please contact our Media Relations team: Sabaina Malik at 416-904-4510 or Rania Walker at 416-258-8953.

Print: ISBN: 978-1482706000

Create Space Publishing – A brand of Amazon.

E-Book: Amazon Kindle

Printed and bound in the Unites States

Interior Design and page composition: Cirro Creative Inc., www.cirro.ca

Jacket design: Alexander Von Ness, www.nessgraphica.com

Disclaimer

The information provided in this book is designed to provide helpful information on the subjects covered, based on my experience as a teacher, healer and facilitator in the healing arts. This book is not meant to be used, nor should it be used, to diagnose or treat any medical condition. For diagnosis or treatment of any medical issue, please consult your physician.

The publisher and author are not responsible for any specific loss, damage or injury occasioned to any person acting or refraining from acting, as a result of the information contained within this publication. Our views and rights are: You are responsible for your own choice, actions and results.

The author and publisher also disclaim any liability to any party for any loss, damage, or disruption caused by errors or omissions, whether such errors or omissions result from negligence, accident, or any other cause.

References are provided for informational purposes only and do not constitute as explicit endorsements.

DEDICATION

Dedicated to all of my clients who have been a part of this "healing" journey with me. You have allowed me to see deeper into the realm of "healing", to see what is possible, to witness how love heals and to experience the infinite flow of pure life force energy in all its magnitude and miracles. Thank you for trusting me to be a part of your healing journey and for your openness to grow beyond where you were.

To everyone I've ever met – however long or brief. You have all been a part of my journey and have assisted with my personal growth, healing and ability to expand to new levels of self-awareness. I thank you all, as you have been my teachers and guides on so many levels! I am who I am today because of you.

To Mr. Timothy Taylor, my grade 9 English teacher. You first introduced me to yoga, meditation and healing! I still have the books you gave to me on Reflexology! You opened my mind to a whole new way of being and set the wheels in motion for the path that I am on today. My life wouldn't be the same if our lives hadn't crossed.

To my loving, supportive and incredibly fun and awesome family! You bring such laughter and joy to my life and I thank you for always loving me, no matter what. I love and appreciate each of you! You allow me to be me.

To my loving and grounded husband who reminds me everyday of the simplicity of healing by remembering who and what I am – The Light! I am eternally grateful for you and the day our paths crossed at Agape in Los Angeles.

PRAISE FOR THE BOOK

"I LOVE this book! Reading the words, doing the exercises and speaking the affirmations is almost like being in the room with Tara, herself. She gently guides us through our resistance, our confusion, and our contradictions, always reminding us that every tool we need to heal - lies in ourselves. From food to exercise, to thoughts and actions, each chapter empowers us to love deeper, listen closer, and expand wider. As a teacher, performance artist, personal trainer and motivational speaker, this book will be an invaluable resource for my students and clients, as well."

Tamara Podemski
Actress, Singer, Dancer
www.tamarapodemski.com

"Tara Antler is a powerful guide accompanying you along the path of self-healing. In "The Healing Manual" she shows you practical methods to access your ability to heal as you learn to communicate with your body. Carried throughout and between her words is a calling of greater personal authority ~ the foundation to regain the authentic balance of mind, body, and spirit. Whether it is physical pain and discomfort, mental anguish or confusion, emotional disturbances ~ times of depression or anxiety, and spiritual crisis or disconnect ~ the real gift of this wonderful book is the sense of personal power that comes from knowing that you can take your health back into your own hands."

Marsh Engle, Author
The Six Essentials: Where Power, Passion & Purpose Connects
www.MarshEngle.com

"The Healing Manual is a timely and empowering book that teaches a set of organic practices to heal our mind, body and soul. Tara provides pragmatic wisdom on living in a healthy and aligned way. A must read book that you will go back to time and time again and want to share with those you love."

Sabaina Malik
Sabaina Malik & Co.
Brand Elevation. PR. Strategic Counsel
Book. Brand. Business.
www.sabainamalik.com

WORDS OF LOVE & APPRECIATION

The content within The Healing Manual has been taught and shared by Tara Antler, with students and clients all around the world over the past ten years. Tara's students and clients experienced many wonderful life transformations, and below you will hear from some of these people.

"The Healing Manual" is a delicious celebration of humanity that teaches us (the reader) that it's our birthright to embody our powerful human potential. Through lovingly crafted chapters, Tara shows us how effortlessly delicious and dis-ease free life can be we give ourselves permission to transcend our perceived limitations and step into the infinite wisdom of our own personal knowing. As a Nurse who works with disease and illness everyday, I find it refreshing to read a book that serves to empower its readers in an aspect of life that, for most, can be so confusing. I believe this book is a powerful tool for anyone willing to engages the content because the language is accessible, the tools are easily implementable, and the outcomes are limited only by one's willingness to "go within".

Morgan Toombs, RN, 2013
Author of Sexy...it's not that serious, www.howtobesexy.tv

"Tara is an angel! She just shines with energy and warmth – she has a true gift of healing. Since I have been working with Tara my chronic fatigue has improved and I have received many unexpected gifts of wisdom, insight and healing messages."

M.M, Life Coach, 2007

"I first met Tara at a workshop in the winter of 2013 where I felt very drawn to her energy, the love radiated off of her! After my first session with Tara I felt as though I had found the person who would help me continue on my path in a way that feels safe and in the supportive and loving way I need. Soon after my first session I made connections for the book I am writing and took a course that I had been dreaming about for a couple of years. I also created my own summer camp! Tara had taught me to love all things in a way that provides understanding to all of life's situations. After every session I feel full of love and a sense of lightness that lifts me forward in my journey. I'm so grateful for crossing paths with such an incredible healer!"

Rebecca Tilling, 2013

"I have gone to Tara for several sessions and attended many classes of hers. One of my favourites was the program, "Living Your Higher Self." What I gained most from taking this course was not only the ability to listen to my own inner voice and intuition, but also the confidence to trust it. The class taught me how to make the best decisions based on my connection to my higher self and what feels intuitively right. My classes with Tara were grounding, inspiring and centering and was an amazing way to gain insight into how to guide myself and navigate my own path in life. Another source of expansion I experienced during the class were the meditations that took me to a whole new realm of spirituality. I was able to delve into a world of meditation which I never thought possible and could not have tapped into on my own. Tara's optimism, support and positive take on everything makes all of her classes foolproof and uplifting. Even a skeptic can benefit as there is absolutely nothing to loose and everything to gain!"

Amy Quick, 2011

Tara's Living Vibrancy course was incredible. The insights it helped me to see in my own life were quite astounding. Tara is an authentic, compassionate, intuitive woman with a connection to Source energy that is stronger and more real than anyone else I have ever met. She has changed my life in so many ways as she helps me to remember who I am when I forget, and it is instantaneous being in her presence. She ignites and lefts up any room she walks into and is a blessing to any group and this world. I am grateful to know her and cannot wait to participate in anything else she has to offer.

Brooke Jillian Yantzi, 2013

TABLE OF CONTENTS

About the Author

Tara Antler grew up in a small town of fifty people in Northern Ontario, Canada, surrounded by an abundance of nature, a loving family, and the continuous flow of people who visited her parent's fishing and camping lodge and resort. She learned from a young age the importance of community, the simplicity of life and the understanding that we are all connected. At the age of fourteen, Tara was introduced to yoga, meditation and other healing modalities by her grade nine English teacher and she quickly took the teachings and began practicing at her favourite place in the world – a large Precambrian Shield rock that overlooks the Ottawa River. Here she learned to connect to a larger energy source, feeling the flow of life force moving through her body, understanding the interconnectedness of all things, people and events and fine-tuning her naturally inherent intuitive abilities.

Both Tara's maternal and paternal linages possessed different intuitive abilities from seeing spirits who had passed on to a strong knowing when a certain person was going to call to being a good "judge" of character. Tara's own abilities surfaced at a young age, seeing and speaking to spirits passed as clear as she would see you or I from the time she was three. Tara recalls always being able to sense people's feelings and often could hear their thoughts. She was also aware that she could change the state of another simply by hugging or loving that person.

Tara left the comforts of the small town and took a massive leap to study Health Sciences at the University of Western Ontario. Her room-mates then commented that Tara should put a jar outside the door and receive donations for the amount of people that would show up, asking for guidance and wanting to talk about their problems. It was clear that helping others was as natural as breathing for her. Tara's favourite subjects – Interpersonal Relationships, Women's Health, Alternative and Complimentary Medicine, and Health and Spirituality – sparked an inner desire to further study Holistic Health Care at the Transformational Arts College in Toronto for two years part-time while she worked full time at the Ministry of Health.

Tara's career in the health and wellness industry has been vast and ever-expanding. After leaving the Ministry she opened her own private practice and healing centre, seeing clients for energy work, Aromatherapy massage, Reflexology and Spiritual Counseling. She then worked in the spa industry learning more about detoxification, luxurious body treatments and retreat programs. From there she consulted at a resort that was transitioning into a retreat centre and was responsible for creating the retreat itinerary, hiring and training spa staff and quickly became the Spa Director. From there Tara's career returned full circle where she was invited to teach at the Transformational Arts College – Aromatherapy, Reflexology, Chakra Studies, Healing with Crystals, Subtle Aromatherapy and Vibrational Arts. From this experience Tara discovered a deep love for teaching and giving back to students!!

Among all the learning, healing and practice, Tara traveled to many different countries and studied many other modalities in the healing arts field from Angel Therapy to Yoga to Theta Healing to Sound Healing. Her heart and intuition always led the way and eventually directed her to California where she found her soul family at Agape International Spiritual Centre and her beloved partner in life, King Gabriel Quincy Collymore. She enjoyed the vastness of it all and the commonality of compassion that weaves us all together. She is passionate about the experience of life on this earth, being of service, creating and living the most amazing life possible, and most importantly showing others how to do the same!

Since 2003 Tara has combined all that she has learned and has a flourishing private healing practice in Toronto, with clients also in Windsor, Ottawa, Northern Ontario, Los Angeles, London England, Mexico, Ireland, France and Australia. Some of Tara's clients include International Opera singers, acclaimed actors, Olympic athletes, and Top 40 artists. She also offers dynamic and loving workshops and classes and continues to expand her platform as her own personal spiritual path evolves. Through her insights and spiritual practices, Tara opens the heart, mind and inner eye of her clients so that they see all that is possible for them and really live into the flourishing life of their dreams with ease, awareness, joy and vitality. They experience a greater love within self, harmonious relationships, a heightened sense of clarity and confidence in their lives, and a deeper connection to their Source energy and life path.

Tara has also always enjoyed writing, as it provides a beautiful platform to share, express and pass along teachings and insights that can really make a different in people's lives.

Tara has been a busy-little-bee, spreading love, clarity and healing everywhere she goes. People feel ignited just by being around her beautiful presence, her hugs are warm and healing, and her light is clear and authentic. Tara is also the Founder of Tara Healing Sanctuary, The Heart of Flourishing, Truth Talk on BlogTalkRadio, Living Vibrancy, and most recently The Academy of LIGHT™. She helps people fall in love, whatever that means for them, helps entrepreneurs grow their business to the next level and helps to create powerfully conscious leaders in the world through a body-mind-spirit approach.

Tara loves living consciously, with an open heart. She believes that we can all shine in our radiance, access more of who we are and really LIVE the LIVES we ARE MEANT TO LIVE!

FOREWORD

"One never needs to say they are Spiritual to be so. It should radiate from you without words and all know it by your presence." DG

There are many people I have had the pleasure of meeting over the 20 plus years in this business and many have touched me by being in their presence. However, few have moved me to a deeper understanding of myself by meeting them as that of Tara Antler.

She writes not from a need to be heard but a desire to be of service and when one writes from that context only good can come from that work. She understands that Self-Love is the key to a successful, full, loving life and with that understanding has put together a book that will be a living source of information to help you transform your life.

This book is not meant to be a cover to cover read, although you can do that, but rather a guide to a deeper understanding of you and the stories you hold that keep you from manifesting the deepest desires of your life.

I am proud to know Tara and for the love that she has taken to pour out HER love into these pages and the healing that I know you will have by applying her wisdom to your lives.

Daniel Gutierrez
Author/Speaker
www.danielgutierrez.com

INTRODUCTION

I wanted to create an easy guide to healing so that people know that they can heal themselves. We are each on a unique and wondrous path, all at different points in our awareness and each with different things going on in any moment. There is no one "perfect" and "only" way to healing. Just as there are many paths that lead to mecca or many roads to take you to your destination, there are many forms of healing that are all wonderful and valid and work, depending on where you are in your journey.

The first three steps anyone can do when "healing" is required is:

1. *Take a pause.*
2. *Tune in to our own self and body.*
3. *Find out what it needs.*

By asking a few easy questions, we begin a fascinating and eye-opening journey inward - discovering more about our inner workings and the interconnection to the world around us. This ultimately guides us to the appropriate level of healing that we require in that moment.

Some great questions to start with are:

❖ *Am I experiencing physical symptoms or imbalances?*

❖ *Am I feeling "off" emotionally?*

❖ *Do I find my thoughts running "a muck" in my life?*

❖ *Am I feeling out of control? Or lack of connection to anything?*

❖ *Am I feeling "cut-off" from life itself?*

Whatever the state, whatever you are moving through, the most important first step is to listen. We were given two ears and one mouth – reflecting the need to listen twice as much as we speak. And when there is an imbalance or resistance, it's a signal to pay attention and go within to listen to what is there and tune into what your being or body is advising you to seek out. Begin by listening to your description of what you're moving/going through. You then have IN-sight as to what requires balance and what to seek out in regards to healing. You will begin to uncover the block or the limiting belief that is showing up or the resistant patterning that is "flaring up" in your body, mind or emotions.

Throughout this book you will discover how easy it is to heal and return to harmony in all areas of your life. You will learn how to listen to your body, its signals and what it's telling you. You will learn how to work with the mind in-stead of being run by it. You will uncover the powerful force of your emotions and how they can let you know what's going on under the surface. And you will receive easy-to-use healing tools that can be used anytime, anywhere and by anyone. I invite you to take this healing journey with me and REMEMBER HOW POWERFUL YOU ARE!

This book does not need to be read in chronological order. You may feel like simply opening up to a random page or ask your higher self to guide you or show the page or information that is best suited at this time. As you listen to your being, body, emotions and thoughts, you may feel a pull to the emotional work or realignment – you would then flip to that section. You can read it how-ever you feel called to. There is no right or wrong way! This is YOUR journey of experience! Let it be a GREAT and WONDROUS one!!!

The modalities that I've mentioned in this book are all modalities that I have studied, experienced personally and have practiced or provided to clients. There are so many healing modalities out there and I'm sure all are wonderful and powerful. However, I can only speak on the ones that I have experienced first hand and know.

When I began writing this book I was in the midst of clearing some major stuff from my body, mind, emotions and spirit. Several months prior to the physical clearing, I had set the intention to KNOW Source or Spirit or God – full on. I wanted know from my own truth and understanding, not from what I've heard, or read, or picked up from others. I was seeking my soul's truth, straight from Source itself. And, so it began. I noticed minor adjustments being made along the way that were shifting my belief systems and eventually releasing most of them. I then noticed my emotional body feeling upset, angry, frustrated and all over the map. As I continued to purge and release and reset, my thoughts were increasingly toxic and depressing and angry. And finally, my body shook up all the old stuff by flaring up like an allergic reaction to myself! I had developed hot, swollen welts and areas all over my head and face. At one point while living in Mexico, my nose was twice its normal size, my upper lip had swelled to three times its normal and my forehead was bulging on one side only. It was horrific, uncomfortable and extremely upsetting. I had a hard time eating. I didn't want anyone to look at me, including my husband, and so I isolated myself inside the apartment for five days and couldn't stop crying.

This cycle of swelling and retreating lasted for a few months, surging and releasing sporadically. I was doing everything to rebalance it. It wasn't until the third round that I actually took some necessary time to reflect and go inward to listen to what my body was telling me!

It was incredible! So much truth began to pour out. So much emotion and thoughts that I had been harboring within me for two years, that also linked to my earliest years in life. Stuff that I had buried that I didn't even realize was there.

There is a time and place for everything in regards to healing. There's a time to reflect, there's a time to dig, there's a time to release, there's a time to ignore. There's a time to purge, there's a time to rest. There's a time to shake it out, there's a time to breathe it out. There's a time to speak it, there's a time to be still. There's a time to get support, there's a time to retreat. There's a time to clear, there's a time to rejoice and celebrate your return. There's a time to set intentions, there's a time to replenish. And there's a time to choose and a time to get reacquainted with the divine and return to pure Spirit or Source and trust and know that all is well and working for your highest and best good!

All of this can be a part of the healing journey. No one journey will be exactly the same.

As I allowed the unfolding of this particular journey, great inspiration sprang up within me that gave way for the creation and expression of this book. It reminded me of times past when I was moving through letting go and walking the healing path. It all came together in such clarity. As I let go, the methods and modalities that surfaced or were remembered came from a space of higher truth and clarity. I hope while reading this book you receive the insights and clarity that you require to bring more balance, healing, transformation and a return to total joy within your life.

Remember to be gentle on yourself. Always love yourself, no matter what is showing up. And have faith that all is happening exactly as it needs to for your expansion and further knowing of truth for you! As you seek truth, be open to receive and trust what presents itself. You are wise and beautiful and perfect, whole and complete as you are. Allow the time for awakening, a return to the fullness of knowing you and your connection to Source, whatever that may be for you!

HOW TO USE THIS HEALING MANUAL

If you choose to use this book as a manual or guide, first tune into your own being, body, emotions, thoughts and mind. Allow the following questions to open the door to your healing journey and give you some insight as to where to begin or what section of the book to flip to. You can use these pages to write down your thoughts, feelings and insights to the questions.

❧ *How are you right now?*

_____

_____

_____

_____

❧ *Is there anything in particular that you want to heal or shift?*

_____

_____

_____

_____

❖ *Is it on a physical, emotional, mental or spiritual level?*

_____

_____

_____

_____

_____

❖ *What is coming up for you?*

_____

_____

_____

_____

_____

❖ *What is/are your being or emotions or body or thoughts telling you?*

_____

_____

_____

_____

_____

❖ *Are you witnessing a physical imbalance? Then you may want to start at the root chakra, chapter 1.*

❖ *Are you feeling really emotional and "off"? Then you may want to go to the sacral or heart chakra, chapters 2 and 5.*

❖ *Are you feeling spiritually cut off or disconnected? Then maybe start at the back of the book and read it backwards, starting with chapter 8 and then move to chapter 7.*

❖ *Are you persistently having negative thoughts or don't like the way the world is showing up for you? Then you may want to skip over to chapter 6 and 7.*

❖ *Or maybe you are feeling all of it, completely out of whack. You may want to just read where ever you feel drawn to. Start somewhere. Take the first step.*

Be your own best detective and case study. Choose to stay detached from the drama or story of what's happening and just notice what's there. Know that you can shift anything and everything that you are witnessing. Think of it as – you are moving through it or through something. It is not permanent. Only a temporary flare up or signal to provide further clarity and growth and expansion.

Your higher or expanded self or being wants you to feel free and open and fully expressed. It wants you to know and live joy and love and perfect health and wellbeing. That is your birth right and natural state of being. Simply learn to let go of what's not serving you and create the space and freedom for your true self to enter in and play!

CHAPTER 1

WE BEGIN AT
THE BASE

*Grounding into & nurturing the body is
ESSENTIAL, like vitamins & water...
do it everyday.*

All of life begins with energy, which streams down into the consciousness of a being and an inspired thought gets created. Energy swirls around this thought and emotional energy becomes present. This emotional charge becomes the rocket fuel to set in motion the physical creation of the thought! From light to vibration to form. This form then requires building blocks to establish a foundation from which to grow and live and come into full fruition in this physical world we call Earth! That's how all of creation comes into form here... from energy to thought to form.

And just like the building of a house, one must first have the idea or thought about building a house. More energy goes into the thought as emotions conjure up further thoughts about what would be nice or lovely to have a part of the house. And so the model of the house gets quickly formulated from the thoughts and emotional feelings about it. Next step is to build it. And, as with any house, one must have a strong and solid foundation from which to build! You don't want any cracks or leaks or wobbling. You want a solid, strong, sturdy and healthy foundation!

This is exactly the same and true for your experience here in the physical body! One must have a foundation or physical vessel in which to live and experience Earth life in and on.

Ancient cultures adored the body and had many beautiful and nurturing practices to love and support and honour the body temple. The Egyptians loved all things euphoric – rose petals, essential oils, milk baths, clothing adorned with jewels and precious stones. They appreciated the physical vessel that they inhabited. Many Native cultures held sacred ceremonies to honour the passing through certain age points along the journey. They also did a lot of smudging and purifying of the physical and energy bodies. Ayurveda medicine is the oldest recorded medicine of our time and it looked at and honoured all levels of the being – physical to spiritual and created a system of eating and activities that were suited for each body dosha or body type that would sustain and create balance and harmony for each individual. And many cultures around the world honoured the five elements, which make up all of life in its many forms – air, earth, fire, water, and ether.

We are interconnected to all of life here on this planet! We are made up of the same elements as everything else on this planet, just in different arrangements and DNA-patterning that give us the different species and forms!

This is one of the reasons working with earth-based medicines and modalities have such a profound effect on us – the herbs, essential oils, crystals, foods and homeopathic remedies maintain their blueprint for what they were intended for, they are directly plugged into Source energy and they haven't forgotten where they come from because they are without ego or separation and therefore are pure life force energy! They remember their essence and powerfully deliver and emit it to us! They actually help us remember on a cellular level WHO WE ARE! And once the body wakes up to this knowing and truth once again, it knows exactly what to do!

Your body has been programmed to do so much! It knows exactly how to run smoothly, function effortlessly and heal miraculously! All it needs is the allowance, free from our own personal resistance from our thoughts, stories and emotions, and it will then receive the innate wisdom from within itself! In every moment you have trillions of cells doing what they know how/what to do, making adjustments along the way, finding balance, and creating perfection all of the time.

The only reason we experience physical pain, imbalances or suffering is because we have gotten our way and we have forgotten who and what we really are. We have created some form of resistance that is stopping or blocking the higher wisdom and functionality. WE ARE THAT POWERFUL! Your thoughts and emotions can influence your physical, sometimes instantly!

Some of the different modalities that belong in this category that can assist with basic physical healing are:

❖ *Plant-based medicines and herbs (herbology).*

❖ *Crystals and healing with crystals.*

❖ *Water, fire, air, earth – based ceremonies like Shamanic or Native healing and ceremonies.*

❖ *Essential oils and aromatherapy.*

❖ *Homeopathic remedies (homeopathy).*

❖ *Bach Flower remedies or other flower essences.*

❖ *Nutritional healing or healing with foods and basic nutrients (nutritional counseling).*

❖ *Ancient food sources – I recently discovered Peruvian herbs and plants like Maca, Camu Camu, Purple Maiz, and Chia seeds. Amazing plants that realign on all levels of being!*

❖ *Massage, bodywork, energy work and reflexology.*

❖ *Grounding meditations.*

❖ *Yoga, Qi Gong and Tai Chi.*

Sandy's Healing Story:

Sandy came to me after a surprising and shocking diagnosis that flipped her life around and catapulted her into a world of healing on every level! She sought out alkaline nutrition, changed her lifestyle, traveled the world in search of healing modalities and eventually found her way to me for Reiki, chakra balancing and energy work. We worked together sporadically over a year doing energy work, healing, thought re-patterning and LOVE mentoring. Her entire life completely expanded and she found new strength flowing through her, a deeper understanding of how her body was communicating to her, and a clear path as to how to help others who have gone or are going through something similar! It made the journey to healing less fearful and more empowering! It was inspiring to be a part of her journey and witness the transformation on a physical, emotional, mental and definitely spiritual level!!!

Here's what she had to say about her journey inward: "Tara Antler opened me up to Reiki and energy work, and its influence on my sub conscious and the healing process. I had been focused on healing my physical body, and I recognized I needed to heal mind, body and spirit – and while I was doing some of this myself, by going to see Tara, she opened me up to further methods of healing through energy work on a sub conscious level. I found that the more I opened up to learning and experiencing energy and taking responsibility for my spiritual growth in the healing process, the more I connected with even more ways that I could expand my intuition and creativity in my life, my studies and in my practice. I have learned ways to embrace energy work in everything that I do now and my life has expanded because of it."

Sandy Cardy
Author of "Shock, Wisdom, Paradise"

Just like a plant that requires clean water and nutrients, feed your body what it needs and what serves it best on all levels (physically, mentally, emotionally and spiritually) and it will create for you the most beautiful, loving and harmonious form!

As much as we are Spiritual beings or energy, we are here in a condensed body of matter or physical suit and it is up to us to take of the suit we arrived in, or not. Why not allow the physical "helpers" help and assist us in achieving or maintaining perfect physical health and wellbeing? Why not give the body everything it needs to function properly! It makes doing the "other work" much easier when our physical body feels strong.

I'm sure we've all noticed what happens if we ignore or negate or neglect the physical – certain imbalances begin to show up or our physical doesn't function at its perfect optimum. However, with a little tender loving care and attention we can get our body in mint condition and tip-top-shape so that we can have a full and wonderful experience while we're here!

And while you are here in a physical body, why not experience some of the nourishing and pampering modalities? A loving, nourishing touch from another is like melting butter – it soothes, relaxes and allows us to let go for a moment in time and just rest. This rest allows for so much healing and rebalancing to occur. Remember, your physical body likes a little love and positive attention too! Just like a newborn baby, the body requires physical touch in order to grow and be healthy. In your adult form, you still require this physical loving touch.

Some of my physical-favourites are:

❖ *Bodywork, like massage, reflexology, lymphatic drainage and shiatsu.*

❖ *Energy work like Reiki, chakra balancing and intuitive healing.*

❖ *All forms and styles of yoga, especially restorative yoga (amazing for the nervous system!)*

❖ *Hydrotherapy – water healing and Watsu (shiatsu in water!).*

❖ *Spa treatments – mud wraps, detox footbaths and salt baths.*

❖ *Dry brushing.*

❖ *Food that tastes GREAT... you know... the stuff that makes you feel GOOD :)*

❖ *Vitamins and supplements that actually absorb into the body (email me for more information on companies/brands that I trust and personal take).*

Don't wait until the body is unwell. Enjoy these physical treatments NOW. Too often we only reach out for bodywork or readjustments when something is wrong or off. What if we made bodywork and balanced nutrition a part of our regular practice and journey? Then the physical body would receive all that it needs at all times!

Step one, taken care of!!!

What is going into YOUR body?

As we look to nutrition and ways of eating, there are several ways to support your body. There's: the "Eat Right for Your Blood Type"; vegetarian; vegan; higher protein; Ayurveda; and many, many, many others. Anything goes. It's not that serious. Simplify it and go back to the basic building blocks and what works for you and your body make-up.

As I was growing up, we ate everything. Then in my mid twenties I became vegetarian, then vegan, then raw, then back to vegetarian with a little of blood type eating and most recently, I had to start eating red meat again. I had an IUD in my body for four years and had no idea that I was building up too much copper in my system. The way to balance out copper is to increase zinc. And guess what the highest absorbable form of zinc is? Red meat. When I did the research, I had every known symptom of a copper toxicity. Who knew? I had never heard of such a thing. So, I had the IUD removed, loaded up on immune and adrenal support for my system, increased my vitamin C and started to eat red meat again. And I have to say… it felt good! I could literally feel my physical cells growing and expanding as they received what they needed! And the allergic swelling that my body had been going through, diminished day by day! My sex drive returned! My mood lifted! I felt grounded and the dizzy spells stopped. I started to feel happy again! My physical was renewed and returning to balance! And I got to grow again by releasing any judgment I was carrying around what was good for the body in regards to lifestyle and diet and discovered a new-found love and appreciation for all that is given to us in the physical form on this planet!

I would say that NOW, I am an "INTUITIVE EATER". I listen to what my body "needs" are and I find a way to provide it.

I would say the most important thing you can do re choosing an eating lifestyle is: to listen to your own body! Your body knows what is right for its type. It takes into consider so many things – your blood, your DNA, your culture, your physical environment, food sources that are available, etc. If you look at eggs one day and your body reacts and you feel no, then don't eat them that day. Maybe in a few days you will look at them and your body feels yes! Then go for it! Sometimes we do not know why we crave and want the foods that we do… trust! Some higher form of communication is going on behind the scenes and all you have to do is listen and trust and then do. It's simple!

And release any thoughts or judgments you may have about any form or style of eating. Judgment is not good for anyone or for any reason and it creates more damage than many of us are aware. It's not enough to just be mindful of the physical food we put into our body. It is equally important, if not more important, to be mindful and considerate of the thoughts we are "feeding" our body. Every thought you have creates a reality and form – positively or negatively effecting the outcome of your physical body.

Love Your Cake… and eat it too :)

Enjoy all of it! If and when you do indulge, simply love it. By doing this, you take the vibration of that food up to a higher vibrational level. Your physical cells respond to energy – energy from thoughts, energy from food, energy from your emotions and energy from the outside world. If food is energy, what kind of energy imprint would you want going in? Fall in love with everything you put in your body... even if "they" say it's not the best for you....

Our physical DNA and cellular needs have not changed that much over the years. There are basic nutritional needs that the body has. Give it what it needs and the innate wisdom of your being and higher self will take care of the rest. You were created or built with a perfect functioning system – it came with the instruction manual built right into the cellular structure and DNA! Your body knows what to do to create and maintain balance. We simply get out of the way, release any resistance and allow it to do what it knows to do.

When it comes down to all of it: choose what feels good to you; choose what resonates with you. Trust your inner knowledge and truth. If you eat something and you feel good on all levels, then great! Does it mean you're going to want to eat that same food every day? Maybe not and maybe so. If you enjoy receiving bodywork, then keep doing it. What ever you choose to do, love it. And if you don't love it or it doesn't bring you joy on some level, then give it up. If something you're choosing is causing you pain or further separation, then give it up and choose something different.

Listening to your body is KEY.

Listen to your body! It has so much to say and is speaking to us all of the time! Sometimes it whispers, other times it shouts.

If you have a broken bone, get it set.

If you have a cold, rest, drink plenty of fluids and increase your vitamin C intake.

If you feel off in your emotions, discover what you can do to ease the discomfort.

*Take some time to slow down and listen to what your body is telling you! There is an entire study on the **Mind-Body Connection** and what it's speaking to us. A few of my favourites here are:*

- ❖ *Louise Hay – Heal Your Life*
- ❖ *Debbie Shapiro – The Mind-Body Workbook*

Your body is always speaking to you and will always tell what's going on under the surface. Be still and love yourself enough to listen. You wouldn't turn your back on a loved one who is trying to tell you something. So, then, don't turn your attention or back away from your own self!

HEALING PRACTICE: "Internal Communication"

You can begin listening to your body at any time. It doesn't have to be just when you're facing dis-ease or imbalance.

Listening anytime – To establish a strong communicative relationship with your body, choose to spend at least five minutes every day to just stop, be and listen to your body. How do you do this? Just like talking to a friend that you love, you begin by asking, "How are you? How are you feeling today? What do you need today? What do you want to eat today? What can I do for you today?" And then just pause, wait and receive. You will get something from your body – pay attention to body sensations, thoughts, feelings or things that pop up in your imagination. All is valid. The more you practice this the stronger your internal communication will become. And then take a step toward what the body is telling you. When you're regularly listening, you will be giving the body exactly what it needs to function with ease and grace and you can often detect energetic imbalances before they settle into your physical body, avoiding pain all together.

Listening in pain – This can be one of the most powerful and insightful times to listen to the body's signals. When we are in pain there is a clear knowing as to what area is "off" or imbalanced. We can see and feel it. We can pinpoint the pain. In this state, again, ask the body, "What is going on here? What do you need? How can I help you?" Pause, wait and receive. It will tell you something. Maybe you get a feeling to go for a walk. Perhaps it tells you to take a bath. Or maybe you feel to call in support from a healer. You can also go a little deeper and ask the body, "Where did this begin? Why are you feeling imbalanced today?" You may receive insights as to what the root of the issue is and take different steps to correct the path, which in turn can alleviate the suffering.

HEALING PRACTICE:
"Divine Intelligence of My Body"

In any physical imbalance or pop-up/flare-up, I call on the Divine Intelligence of My Body to enter in and do what is necessary for health, rebalancing and restoration. I then imagine or feel or see energy traveling into my body and activating or turning on this intelligence. The billions of cells in my body receive the signal and take care of the rest!

And when you're not sure what's going on – we all go through moments like this – reach out and get support. Again, when you're building a house, you most likely would be building it on your own would you? You would have support, people who can assist with the perfection of it! Your body and being is just as important. Reach out and get support and assistance when you need it!

That's what healers and health practitioners are here to do with you! You are not alone on this journey! Let someone light the way and hold your hand for a little while!

Then, when the physical body is tended to, you have more space and freedom to explore what's really going on under the surface.

The Energetics of Grounding are as natural as breathing… aahhhh…

Next stop on my healing journey was to take care of the energetic grounding and return to the simplicity of nature! I needed to return to the basics – air, earth, fire, water, and ether. I needed to be held. I craved reconnection.

And as I did, I found my roots again. I planted my feet into the sand, let the water glide over the tops of my feet, opened my eyes and arms to the night sky and breathed in the pure breath of life. There is so much love and healing that occurs when we return to nature and the basic building blocks of life. If you let it, nature will completely cradle you and restore you back to balance! Because it knows its connection to Source. It remembers and wants us to remember also! It knows harmony and balance and knows how to stay grounded so that it can reach up to the heavens and receive the Source energy from above and let it travel down through our being to replenish and refill us on all levels!

HEALING PRACTICE: "Get Grounded"

A great grounding practice that I use all of the time is this:

Before you get out of bed in the morning, plant your feet on the floor, close your eyes and breathe. With every inhale imagine drawing in life-force energy into your body and with every exhale imagine sending this energy down your body, through your feet and into the earth. Imagine this energy extending into the earth itself and creating roots, just like that of a tree, extending in all directions. Feeling firming grounded and ready to begin this new day being as present as humanly possible!

Any time throughout the day you can use this visualization and imagine your roots in the earth again. Once you are grounded, you are free to extend up and into the world as openly as you want to be.

New Healing Habits for Building a Strong Foundation:

1. *Create a "grounding" practice during any time of change, creating the new, healing or rebalancing. Think about a yoga class and how powerful standing and standing-balancing postures are. You want to be sturdy like a tree, deeply rooted into a strong foundation, knowing that you are beautifully supported on every level as you expand and grow upward and onward!*

2. *Your body is a perfectly engineered vessel that carries the brilliance and magnitude of your Soul! Treat it as the most precious, beautiful temple you've ever laid eyes on! As you love it, it will love you back by running with ease and grace!*

3. *Remember, your body is never against you or doing anything "to you". It is neutral... waiting to receive direction through your thoughts and your spiritual self as to how to be, how to show up, how to function and what to create. Create a daily practice of feeding your body healthy thoughts and it will in turn create a physical experience that matches that.*

CHAPTER 2

THE SACRED OR SACRAL DANCE OF LIFE

Our VITALITY is VITAL.

As my healing journey continued to unfold and release, and after I took some much needed time to reconnect to self in nature and find my roots, I felt a wonderful surge of energy circling from my pelvis and sacral area! It was lovely to feel so much life force and raw energy stirring within me once again! All of life seemed to buzz around me in response! The creative flow opened and the words of expression just poured out like smooth liquid gold! I felt alive! I felt vital! I felt happy! I felt awake!

It was only after I got grounded and allowed my body to be held and nurtured that the life force within could activate and actualize once again! And I remembered how important this energy was to our vitality. When we feel creatively in the flow, we feel more alive, we feel more "charged", we feel more awake and present in the world and we feel MORE of WHO WE ARE!

The sacral chakra is the wheel of emotional experience in the physical form! It is a powerful center for creative energy just waiting to be utilized and engaged in and brought to life in this physical world! And our entire being is here to create… we are infinitely creative beings… the creative life force is meant to be alive, well, active, and utilized! It is also the energetic pathway for us to connect with others in this earth experience and share intimacy and feelings.

When this chakra or area of our experience is imbalanced, we may feel "cut-off" from the world or other people, we may feel "quiet" in the area of sexual expression, we may feel flat or lifeless or we may feel stagnant or stuck. Sound familiar? If we aren't using this energy in healthy creative ways, life feels as though it stops, we feel less vital, less alive and we actually begin to deteriorate or age. We are meant to create and when we do we feel alive and vibrant!

So many of today's population experiences imbalances in this area – due to sexual pains and traumas, suppressed creativity and over emphasis on the mind and analytical, complacency, boredom or seizing to imagine, wonder or create, confusion as to sexual preference and imbalanced or skewed imaging about our body, intimate relationships and what is acceptable.

Like any part of body, being or energy system, we can regain clarity, balance and flow by making a few small and easy changes. And most often the simplest, easy activities are the most impactful!

Ways to move, open, awaken or support the sacral:

❖ *Playful Dance.*

❖ *Music, singing, chanting.*

❖ *Easy, gentle Movement.*

❖ *Hips circles and hoola-hoops.*

❖ *Yoga – especially Kundalini Yoga.*

❖ *Create something – gardening, cooking, painting, arts and crafts, write, design or anything else that you find creative in.*

❖ *Step outside and connect with nature! Nature is filled and overflowing with creativity and abundance! Change is occurring all the time all around us. This reminder wakes us up internally!*

❖ *Do something new! Expand your horizons and go somewhere new, do something new, explore and discover something fresh and new! This again opens us up by activating our senses, awakening our imagination and stirring our creative experience of life!*

❖ *Water – swimming, floating, taking a bath. During this time, get to water – a lake, a river, a stream, or the ocean – especially being on the water, on a boat, on a dock, or even in a hammock. The gentle swaying and rocking motion will remind you on a deep cellular level of the womb. It will make it easier to return to that place of stillness, comfort and flow. Let yourself be rocked and held. Feel your body surrender to the sway of the water. Feel into the soothing nature of the water. Feel your body let go. This is what it felt like in the womb when you were a baby. Let yourself return to that beautiful, perfect, warm, safe space. And then just let go. Release... Relax... and let it all melt away... Trust... Release... Let go...*

Return to Life and feel the BUZZ of it again!

It's not a fun feeling when you have no sex drive or desire to connect to your partner or to life, or to even begin to think about creativity or creating something when nothing is moving in that region. It's seems impossible.

And as women, we give and give and give and we've also learned how to do and do and do. The imbalances have become an epidemic. And it is essential to re-balance and allow the softness of life to return and to give yourself permission to be held and supported!

This supportive and nourishing time is essential to any healing and rebalancing. It allows the time and space necessary to re-center ourselves in our body and just like being cradled when floating on water, we have the full feeling sense that we are held and that all is well. We remember that we can let go for a moment and surrender into the safety of the womb to allow the rebirthing and recreation of self to take place.

This time of the healing phase is what many refer to as the void or going into the cave. It is an essential time of recreation, recalibration and rebirthing. This is a really great time for meditation! Meditation allows you the space to feel held, nourished, supported and perfectly still. It allows the space for letting go and to just be, with nothing to do and nowhere to go. You get to just be. And in this be-ingness you get to return to your connection to Source as a beautiful byproduct! Your nervous system receives nourishment, your circulatory system flows with ease and grace, your mind gets to take a vacation, your emotions get to calm, your breathing gets to return to its full breath, and every system and organ in your body receives everything they need to return to optimal functioning!

Every time I move through my stuff and arrive at this phase of healing, I find myself wanting to meditate several times a day or just sit and breathe and take in the beauty of the world. Many times I don't want to do anything. I just want to be and breathe and reconnect to the raw energy of creation all around me. I receive so much from this simple and easy method or modality.

Naps and sleeping are also great during this phase! You are a new baby who is growing… and babies sleep A LOT! When you rest, you are integrating all of the release work, all of the new space that you've created and all of the new energy that is pouring in for and to you. It is a time to receive the fullness of your being again! To be rebirthed, brand new, refreshed, revitalized! Wouldn't you want to be present for that!?!

How to "Get" There...

Let yourself sit in the quiet magic of this phase. Birth is such a miracle of life expressing itself and coming into the world! Be a witness to your own birth and miracle!!!! It will be one that you DO remember!

Think about a baby in the womb, growing and developing to maturation and readying itself to present to the world. We go through the exact same thing when we shed, release and let go. We shed so much that we are pure and fresh, like a newborn baby. This is a time to refresh and ready yourself for the world again. If we leave the womb time too soon we can often feel over sensitive and raw. Which can lead to overwhelm and shock and then we just want to retreat even further or we flare up our emotions as a form of protection to let the people in our external world know, to back off, leave me alone, get away from me. This is often very harsh and painful for self and for the loved ones on the receiving end. They don't understand what happened or what they did to make you behave this way. They take it personally, when really it's not personal at all. It's simply something you are moving through and wish that you could explain it to them so that they'd understand.

And maybe they will and maybe they won't. Sometimes the best option is to let your family and friends know that you're moving through something and that you may be in your cave or cocoon or withdraw or hide away from the world for a little while. It's okay. You can say to them, "I'm okay and I will resurface. I simply am recreating and recalibrating and need space and time to develop my new skin/self."

Most people will understand, as we have all been there. Find a way to comfortably express this and you will receive what you are asking for with ease and grace. Then you are free to sleep, rest, play, go within and not feel pressure for needing to be "on". This is exactly what retreats are designed for – to give you that isolated, away from it all feeling and space to let go, surrender, be held and regenerate yourself. If you haven't experienced a retreat as yet, I highly recommend one!!!

You'll know when it's time to resurface again and return to the rest of the world. You'll know because you will have become more tuned in to you and what your being and body needs and is saying. When we are surrounded by other people, it can be very loud and we often can't hear ourselves. The cocooning time allows you to find your inner voice again and to listen inside instead of out.

You'll know it's time to rebirth yourself because you'll feel a sense of renewal and recharge and new energy surging through your body. You may feel drawn to reach out to friends and family and wonder how they are. You may feel like being around people or celebrating or moving instead of resting. This would be a great time to go dancing or learn to play a new instrument! You may feel differently about the world and self and people.

Michelle's Healing Journey:

I love this story as it is a true testament of the power of words, creative expression and emotional connection through sharing when we are going through "stuff". In writing my IN-sight (newsletters) I always set the intention to be authentic and transparent on all levels… this includes with my own "stuff" and when the grit hits the fan. We all move through things in life and I always want my clients and students to know that I'm with them. I had shared something painful that I had recently gone through and received the following feedback from a woman I met many, many years ago. I was amazed to witness the impact it had on her, how it activated her, and inspired her to take action in response. We never know who will be lifted or elevated by what we're willing to share or put out there and be honest about in our own life. I fully felt the interconnectedness between people regardless of how much time or space exists. When we allow healing to occur, it occurs and opens the gates to creative flow and expression.

Here's what she had to say: "Moments of peace seem to flood me when the sharing of your words hits my eyes. Absolute calm during the storm. Profound are your words as they find my heart. It is a time in my life where your words support. I would like to accept your healing words and share my appreciation. Discover the beauty of life. You speak of the veil and somewhere inside me has fluttered up, it is my time to recognize. Winter is over inside. Thank you Tara. You have entered my life many moon cycles ago, thank you!"

Michelle Tessier

When YOU do resurface, remember to continue to take time for self every single day! Time for nourishment and to stay connected to self and Source! You want to think and be like the turtle, not the hare and go running all around again. You want to keep your batteries recharged and healthy and well and connected to Source!

Below you will find some of my favourite Sacral tools of transformation…

HEALING PRACTICE: "I LOVE myself!"

Find time every day for self-love and nourishment. It may be a bath, a long walk outside, your favourite latte, time to journal or read a book, throwing yourself a dance party in your living room, listening to your favourite music, watching movies that carry you into the imagination, painting, writing, drawing, singing, playing… things that take you into feeling GREAT and where you feel a balance of input and output. When we are burnt out, imbalanced in the areas of our life, tired or over-whelmed the body shuts down and our natural flow of hormones de-creases which affects every part of normal feeling, including lowering our sex drive or limiting our ability to feel alive or passionate. Even if you only have ten minutes a day to spend on loving you, the effects are extraordinary! Your body/being begins to feel the love, it then feels taken care of and supported and begins to reset in the rest and play. And your hormones come back online!

HEALING PRACTICE: "Dance Your Way into Life!"

I LOVE dance and dancing! There are many forms and styles. Choose one that resonates with you and gets your body flowing in its natural rhythms. You can't do dancing wrong. Dance in a way that feels good to you! If it feels good, you'll feel good and everything else will elevate! Start in your living room, put on some music you love and rock away!

HEALING PRACTICE: "Rhythm Reconnection."

Drumming, drum circles and sound healing circles are a powerful way to shake out the cobwebs from your sacral and reconnect you to your natural rhythm and the rhythm of the earth and your heart beat. The constant rhythm of sound reminds us of the womb and all of the sounds we experienced while there. It allows us to feel at ease and know that we are held once again. Sound is extremely transformational! I highly recommend going to a drum circle or sound healing event… or take some drumming lessons… highly therapeutic!

HEALING PRACTICE: "The Food of the Gods."

Chocolate!!! I know it seems cliché, but I LOVE chocolate and it immediately puts me in my sensual body. Take your time while you enjoy it… smell it, feel it, let it melt in your mouth and savour the aromas of every piece! Plus, it has amazing health benefits like major antioxidants for anti-aging!

New Healing Habits for Dancing with the Sacral:

1. *You are a naturally creative being! That's what you came "here" to do... to experience life through all creation (yours and others). Continue to create and you will continue to feel alive and vibrant and flowing!*

2. *When you feel depressed in this sacral area, take some necessary time to receive! No doing, no giving, no action. Just be and receive! This will do wonders for your entire being! You will feel alive, refreshed and new happy hormones will flood your system ready to emerge and serve and create again! Remember, life is about balance! Receive ~ Give ~ Receive ~ Give ~ Receive ~ Give. It's like a beautiful continuous wave. When you allow this flow balance becomes the byproduct.*

3. *Don't be afraid of the dark (the void). The void or cocoon phase is essential when resetting, resting and rebalancing. We go inward to reset and recalibrate so that we can rebirth and resurface anew! Be with it, accept it when it comes and surrender to the quiet stillness that will soon release you to the external world again.*

CHAPTER 3

REGAINING & RECLAIMING PERSONAL POWER

The battle of the "Wills".

Within your solar plexus exists a complex duality that is always asking for balance. Here exists your personal will – the ability to choose for yourself, your personal power. Connected to the expanded spheres of your energy field exists your higher will – the ability to drop-down inspiration, inspired action and new creative thoughts or paths that are in alignment with your expanded self, higher truth and soul knowing using the power of your powerhouse solar plexus. And somewhere mixed up in the earth body and experience exists your ego will – the part of you that wants to play small, keep you where you are, doesn't like or want change and will do everything in its "power" to override your other will abilities by stripping you of your power.

Considering all of this, it's no wonder why we feel conflicted, uncertain, confused and at odds with ourselves… we literally have a battle of will-power going on that never really ends until the day we depart this physical form we call life.

So, then what can we do to make this battle seems a little more peaceful and resolved? The trick is to become aware of what's there and the quality of these different will-powers at play and then align ourselves with where we feel the best. (I go into more detail about this in Chapters 5 and 6).

Your personal will thoughts will want certain things, you will want to make certain choices based on what you know or what experience has shown you. You will tend to feel neutral… it's neither this or that. For example, choosing to brush your teeth a certain way at a certain time. Or choosing what food to eat. Or choosing which house to live in based on what you like or want.

Your higher will thoughts will feel rushing, like waves of insight or inspiration and you will feel a pull or calling toward a certain thing, person or path. Sometimes its pull is so strong that we feel like it's taking us without us doing much at all… we are along for the pleasure ride! And we always end up in an amazing place, far beyond what our planning or personal will could take us. You will tend to feel uplifted, joyful, happy, inspired and blissful. For example, you feel a call to travel to a certain place for no particular reason, there's no logical knowing behind it, and yet you know you HAVE to go. And as you go along, everything just lines itself up perfectly!

Your ego will thoughts are often filled with confusion, fear, lack, limitation, the "buts" of life, the doubting mind, etc. You will tend to feel sluggish, low energy, not inspired, more confused and no good at all. For example, you may want to date a certain person and you feel good about it and all is lining up and then you hear in your head, "Ya, but it can't be this easy. Something's about to drop. He/She can't be this great. When's it going to get bad? Maybe I don't deserve things to be this easy." Sound familiar? We are constantly bombarded by this negative, self-sabotaging mind and we often lean towards it and listen to it or believe it as the truth (false truth).

Here's how you discern the difference between these wills… if the thoughts, direction and action have you feeling good then it's all good. If you start feeling bad, or you felt great and then whammo you had a false truth thought and feel bad, then it's the trickster of the ego doing its crazy dance. And you really don't have to dance with it.

You can choose which thoughts to align yourself with or listen to. Each time you choose a higher thought, you step into your higher or divine power and higher truth once again! And this is where we want to be! Not controlled by the ego's will... rather in the flow and in harmony with the higher will. There more we allow the higher will to govern our life, the more our life becomes enjoyable and pleasurable and things just seem to work out!

Your personal Energy Source is POWER-FULL like the SUN.

As we travel through the chakras and our experience of life, we arise from the restful cocoon, receiving all that was given back to self while rebirthing, and feeling a renewed sense of energy! This is the time in the healing journey to power up from inside! You want to stay replenished and bright like the sun. It is the time to re-emerge and step into your new found internal power and strength. It takes a lot of courage to walk through the phases of awakening, awareness and healing. Take a moment to acknowledge how amazingly powerful you really are!

Personal power in its balanced state looks and feels like standing in one's personal truth, feeling trust run through the experience at all times, and knowing when to move forward and exert energy and when to relax and be still to receive energy. There is a beautiful dance of fire within. Sometimes we feel the roar of the fire and are ready to move forward, other times we feel the quiet, steady burning of embers deep within, conserving energy while being still and open and ready for what's next. In power-balance, we know when to use our power for our life, to "power-up" an idea or action into form, we never over-power or control another as we trust that he/she has his/her own power source also, and we trust in the flow of life that is happening for us, not against us. We feel confident, secure, trusting, clear, worthy and strong. We know who we are and we stand fully in this truth while still being like the tree of flexibility. We are open and not closed and radiant like the sun!

HEALING PRACTICE: "BE the SUN."

Build your internal energy through the power of your thoughts. Sit in meditation or stand outside in the fresh air and either imagine or feel the sun's radiance shinning down on you. Feel its warmth and acknowledge its strength and reach from so far away. It is so powerful and beautiful its fullness. Imagine or feel the sun's light moving into your body and filling up your solar plexus area (upper abdomen, above your belly button). Imagine or feel your own body awakening to your own personal SUN or power center. See it bright like the sun, filling you up first and then warmly and perfectly radiating out from your body and into the space around you. Know and remind yourself that you are in harmony with the rest of the world and all people. Begin to see or imagine each person as having their OWN SUN TOO – radiating just as powerfully and beautifully as yours.

Reclaiming and regaining your personal power really comes back to choice. Along the way, for various reasons, you gave your power away. Maybe it was something that someone said to you that hurt you and at the same time he/she seemed stronger or more powerful than you and your little mind agreed that you were weaker. Maybe something physically distressing happened where you felt as though you didn't have a choice and therefore someone took your power away. Or maybe you feel you weren't heard or acknowledged growing up and therefore felt diminished. What ever the reason, what ever the story, what ever the pain… we've all been there and we all know what it feels like to give our power away or have it taken (although, no one can ever REALLY take our power… we choose to give it over or up) or feel powerless.

In this moment, I encourage you to take a stand within yourself, within your life. What ever the circumstances of powerlessness are, imagine gathering them all up and make a choice to clear or be done with all of that. The past no longer defines or confines you. The pains of the past and the people associated with any of this no longer control you, no longer have power of you. You are making a choice NOW to be complete with the powerless pains of the past. Take a deep breath and let it all go! Breathe it out NOW!

You are taking a stand. You are choosing to reclaim your power. Imagine all of the leaking energy from the past be drawn back into your body, along with all the learning that came from each situation. You are reclaiming your power. You are calling back your power... the power you had once given away and let seep out. You now know how valuable that energy is and you now know how valuable you are... and therefore you require all of your energy back in your body... right here, right now. With every inhale breathe your own life force and energy back into your body, back into your solar plexus area......And consciously choose to stand in your truth and power. And with compassion, release all the rest. Always release with love and compassion. It's so much easier than resentment or judgment.

How do you feel now?

In any moment, at any point in YOUR life, YOU can reclaim YOUR power. It is yours to share, give, let go of, utilize or reclaim. It is YOUR choice. Always. As you reclaim your power YOU become more confident, self-accepting, self-loving, worthy and responsible. You begin to know fully that no one can make you do anything, or make your feel anything, or even that he/she is doing anything to you. Things happen and we can release the taking it personally and see it for what it really is... contrast, learning, expansion and growth. This way of being saves so much time and energy. We actually get stronger with each passing conflict or situation. We stop blaming others, we stop pointing fingers, we stop judging others, and we stop the pushing or pulling. And we truly begin a journey of regaining our life force and true power in the purest sense... filled with honour, respect, love, compassion and appreciation. We begin using our power through the openness of our heart! This is the stuff that literally moves mountains!

HEALING PRACTICE: Positive Power Statements

Now that you've reclaim your power and you are standing powerfully again in your energy and physical body, it is a great time to create Positive Power Statements! These are statements that are created in the present tense that reinforce who you are and how you want to feel and be or show up in the world! For example: "I AM strong, healthy and vibrant!" or "I AM compassionate and loving towards myself and all beings."

I like to use the I AM statement to begin as it reaffirms to me that I AM creator and I AM creating this experience! A total reclaim of personal power!

What are your Positive Power Statements for today?

_____

_____

_____

_____

_____

_____

_____

Accepting the bear within...

Now, I want to touch on anger and frustration for a moment. These emotions are powerful and can create the heat and flame that we need to move us forward and create change. They can also heat us up to the point of burning us, creating welts, pimples, skin flare-ups, indigestion, ulcers and other inflammatory ailments.

Many people have been taught that anger is bad and shouldn't be expressed. Like any emotion trying to find its way out to emote, anger too will find a way out. I have tackled anger from all angles – I've denied it, suppressed it, pretended, and hidden it. And every time it found a way out, often exploding out of me like a violent volcano erupting everywhere and on anyone in my path, and often showing on my body. I definitely had to pay attention then…I couldn't hid anymore. I then attempted to let it just rip and it did, overly expressing everywhere, when ever and on those closest to me. This left behind a path of destruction so immense that there were times I didn't think I would be able to repair the damage.

I eventually got to a place where I recognize the feeling, allow it to be there, accept it for what it is, and without judgment ask it to teach me, "Show me what I'm missing. Show me the learning. What's at the core." I let it speak, I let it teach me, I let it empower me. And then if there's excess emotion still bubbling, I find a way to physically release it through walking, working out, kick boxing or writing. The moment I feel frustration I do my best to catch it and communicate with it before it escalates to anger. Often anger and frustration are simply there to let us know that we need to make change and our being can't take the old any longer. It literally pushes us out of our center and fires us up to make necessary change NOW.

There are many ways to allow this emotion space to breathe and express without creating harm to self or others. It's important to find balance with these emotions, just like any other. And to accept what is coming up and then allow it to teach you rather than burn you.

Clearing the Fear that "makes" us small.

On the other side of the solar plexus spectrum is fear. You know…that little something inside us that causes us to shrink and shrivel and curl up in fear and debilitation. Fear is simply another emotion to let us know that we are growing or on the verge of expanding into a greater version of ourselves! The little self (or ego) doesn't like change and wants to keep us small. So it will do everything in its "power" to limit us, scare us or keep us exactly where we are… FROZEN. However, who's really holding the torch of fire within? Your little self or your expanded self? The choice again is yours to make. You can choose to take back the fire within and use it to light your way, to light the darkness and then there's really nothing to fear. Your higher, expanded self can then guide the way as you take each step forward into new horizons! Change is so very exciting! It stretches us, expands us as we become more of who we really are!!!

If we let fear override our power we can often feel diminished, stuck, low energy, limited, controlled or small. That bright beautiful sun actually becomes blocked by fear clouds that eventually cause the rays of light to withdrawn and hide within… like a scared mouse hiding in a dark hole afraid to ever come out again. Is this how any of us really want to live or experience life? Definitely not. If left in this space for too long we can experience physical imbalances like sluggish digestion, depression, decrease in the proper hormone release, back pain, kidney imbalances, sadness, lack of vitality and worse case diabetes.

Fear can also create a lot of stress in the emotions and body. And stress is like a direct attack on the body, throwing it into a hyper sensitive state in which everything has to work harder. This in turn uses up more of our vital life force energy that we could otherwise be using for creative ideas, projects and ways of living our life. By now we have all heard of the impact that stress has on our overall wellbeing… it depletes, ages, diminishes and over-stimulates us on every level. When we can free ourselves from stress and the causes of stress everything feels better! Our organs function better, our digestion soothes and flows with ease, our hormones level out and our general state feels more balanced.

You can easily clear any fear by first acknowledging that it's there. Face your fear... don't let it control you. By seeing it, accepting it and loving it anyways you take your power back. If you face the shadows with light and acceptance (and love) there's no longer any darkness to fear, let alone see.

Next step, don't take it (the fear) so seriously and become a little more nonchalant (unless you're really being attacked by a bear or something... then seriously run and let your fight-or-flight mechanism kick in). Begin to remember and realize that the fear is there to let you know you're growing! Relax into it by breathing and feel your body let go just a little... the same feeling as floating in a body of water. In order for your body to float you have to let go and trust that you will be held and all will be well. How did you know that you could float? You trusted, tried it, and did it! When you do this once, you build a new belief that you ARE supported and if you were supported once before you can be again. Trusting and relaxing into any fear gets easier and easier.

Then imagine lifting your solar plexus sun energy to your heart and allow courage to flow through. Once you feel expanded and like you can breathe again you are ready to take a step in the direction of the fear. Know that you will not die... that's the BIG fear by the way... that keeps us stuck... that somehow change equals death. And maybe on one level your old way of being is dying off, however, as with any release of the old, new life is reborn and recreated!! You will expand so much by accepting the change that is knocking at your door! And when change knocks it is because you are fully ready for the new to come through. Each time you release and rebirth you get stronger and healthier and happier and more vibrant!!!! Who wouldn't want that!!??

Here are some other POWER-FULL tools to engage, awaken, rebalance and reclaim your SOLAR plexus:

❖ **Qi Gong.** *A physical and energetic practice where you tangibly begin to feel and harness the energy of the elements or Qi around you and bring it into the body! It builds life force energy within the physical structure. We begin to feel more grounded in our power.*

❖ **Yoga and Fire Breathing.** *Amazing ways to stay balanced and fluid while engaging in increasing fire or heat in the body!*

❖ **Exercise (of any sort).** *Will generate heat when we need a boost and also release excess heat (often displayed as anger or frustration – all solar plexus emotions) that has accumulated in the body. Either way, be sure to drink plenty of water to rebalance the fire energy!*

❖ **Meditation and visualization.** *I LOVE meditation. You will see meditation listed in every section! For me, meditation is an essential element – like water and vitamins – it is a fundamental practice that we can use any time, for anything and anywhere!*

Create a new space for your energy to flow.

This may be the time where your new creative ideas and energy will spring up and want to find physical expression and form. You may feel to take action steps towards the manifestation or creation of them. You may begin to make powerful changes in your life and world. You may feel inclined to take tiny steps or leaps and bounds. You feel strong and healthy and well! You feel ready to move forward. You feel empowered within, equipped with the tools to action any change or idea. You feel powerful, as though you can take on the world!

And yes, you can! And so you shall!

Take one step at a time. And be present to every step. Now is also an amazing time to create a plan of action or an idea map of where you want to go and what steps to take so that you can stay focused and on the path you are creating for yourself. There are many ways to create an action plan or goal set. When you do, please allow for flexibility in your planning, as many times your higher self has an even better plan for you… that's way easier, more fun and incredibly expansive!!! Always allow from for leeway and spontaneous change. Too much control can create tightness is areas and places we don't want and can create stress and anxiety. Too little responsibility or action can create severe detachment, complacency and no movement, expecting everything to just show up for us. We want to create balance in our power center – knowing when to move forward and when to relax into the flow. It's like breathing.

And know that you do not have to any of it alone. So many people are trying to do this journey alone or pushing through life thinking that they have to get it right, they have to prove something, or if they want things done right might as well do them yourself attitude. This is quite restrictive and isolating, not to mention exhausting and frustrating… so much of our personal energy and power is over-exerted in this way.

We are surrounded by so many other people/souls who are here with amazing gifts to share. Imagine if we would allow everyone to live their gifts, thrive in what they love and contribute to one another. We would all feel supportive, honoured and respected. We would feel empowered. When you feel the pull to reach out, reach out and ask for help. There is great growth in being open to receive support, both for you and for the person offering his/her gifts. We then allow others to stand in their respective truth and power! By trusting in another we remember that we have so much loving support around us and that it can show up in all sorts of ways. All you need to do is relax and ask.

And regarding "getting it right", what if you can't fail? What if you couldn't get any of this "wrong"? What if there's nothing to prove? What if you didn't have to push your way through life or push your beliefs onto others? What if everyone was free to experience life his/her own way and that way is perfectly orchestrated for that person? What if you're entire experience here on earth is to experience life…in the way and fashion that you'd like to experience it? Simple. Wouldn't that allow for so much freedom for each of us? It would certainly lift the "shoulds" of life, release the pressure we place on ourselves and others, remove the fear of failure, and dissolve any judgment we place on ourselves or others. Can you imagine all the extra energy you would have that is no long wasted or exerted on stress and worry and doubt and failure and fear? What would you do with that extra energy? Imagine all the energy you would have and feel that could be utilized to create and flow and dance with life? Imagine how alive and vibrant you would feel?

Imagine that you are this brilliant energy source that knows its creative power and knows exactly how to action it in the world......What would life look like for you then? How much can you shine? How far can your light and internal power reach? Remember, the only limits that exist are the ones that you create or agree to in your own mind. You are infinite and powerFULL!

Matt's Healing Story:

I co-facilitated a beautiful and empowering workshop with several of my students called "Stepping into the LIGHT" The energy and insights that flowed through that day awakened everyone in the room to a new knowing that we/they are IT – creators! And with that comes great power!

Here's what one of the students had to share after his experience in the workshop: "I want to give you a big "Thank You!!" for your amazing facilitation of the Stepping Into Your Light workshop last weekend. Prior to joining the workshop I was drowning in my own negativity and self-doubt around several things in my life, and certainly not connected to my own 'light'. It was during your introduction at the beginning of the day (a simple 20 minute talk) that everything shifted for me Spontaneously!! You reminded me of who I really am, that BEing light is a choice, that I can 'clear my crap' instantaneously, that karmic debt is an antiquated frame of reference that doesn't serve a higher purpose any more, and that I can choose to let go of all that does not serve me... right now!! You reminded me of my quantum biology, and showed me how to feel it, tap into it, be it, and most importantly live it consciously and consistently moving forward in my life... all within the first 20 minutes of the workshop!!! Everything after that was icing on the cake:) I can't thank you enough for everything you are, everything you represent, and the impact you have had on the quality of my life. You're weaving miracles, girl;) You are a gift to this world, and I can't wait to read your new book!!"

With light and love, Matt W,
Toronto Canada
Advancing the Art of Self-Evolution!!

Cleansing the body to match the vibration.

On a physical level, this may be a good time to cleanse the body. You will have more life force energy to actively cleanse and detoxify. You are stronger now to take on such a task.

There are many cleanses out there – from liver to kidneys to skin to digestive. It is important to speak with a health care practitioner about cleansing to find out what type of cleanse is best suited for you and what you need to do to accomplish it. Remember, be gentle on yourself, stay away from aggressive cleanses that can shock your system – they can weaken the body and its systems, and you want to stay in POWER or empowered and strong. The way to do that – gentle, easy, longer cleanses are generally better for the body and mind. Plus, the gentler approach keeps you in a balanced state of power and steers you clear of going in an aggressive direction.

You may even find that ailments like indigestion, heartburn, insomnia, adrenal fatigue, back pain, IBS or stomach issues all disappear! Why? Because you're open and allowing the flow of your own energy to provide power and life force energy to your body causing healing to occur! Zero resistance!

Also, you may feel to begin or return to your workout routine. You may have a lot of energy that it feels as though it has to move! Now is the time to move! To be active! To pump this new energy into motion. Working out, lifting weights, fitness classes, yoga, workout dancing, mixed martial arts, listening to music that pumps you up, that moves you and grooves you are powerful ways to work with and flow with this new-found energy!

New Healing Habits for Reclaiming YOUR Power:

1. *You are more powerful than you could ever imagine! By acknowledging and accepting ALL of you (every aspect, characteristic, trigger, reaction and response), there is nothing left to fear or run from. You literally liberate yourself from the grips of the ego-will!*

2. *By reclaiming your LIGHT, you reclaim your POWER! You are so much more than these physical bodies… you are infinite creative energy and life force just waiting to spring into action!*

3. *Even the physical imbalances that show up from time-to-time cannot control or stop you. You are much more powerful than that. These aliments are simply ways that your body is communicating to you so that you can become empowered again and consciously choose the reality in which you would like to share your energy with.*

4. *Controlling another, or trying to control every little detail of life, is like being controlled by the ego-will… it doesn't feel good, it costs you a lot of energy, and it takes away power instead of lovingly supporting, honouring and amplifying/magnifying it. Learn to let (it) go.*

5. *Reclaiming your personal power is as easy as saying YES to anything. By choosing YOU, by saying YES to all of who you are (yes, all of it), you step into a place so magnificent, so powerful that no-thing can knock you over. There is nothing to hide from, nothing to be scared of. By standing in full awareness you actually receive more energy and vitality because you are radiating from your FULL self! And this energy can carry you through anything!*

CHAPTER 4

RETURN TO THE HEART & REMEMBERING LOVE

The nature of the HEART is LOVE!

When we are moving through ANYTHING of imbalance our heart chakra really takes a beating. Because we often feel locked off, cut off, disconnected and experience emotional flare-ups that make us want to separate from people and self and we have just undergone an intense inner reflection or picking apart phase, our heart is not functioning at its optimum. The heart then feels low, sad, and its physical functions suppress slightly like a weakened immune system.

Any time you see an imbalance that is related to your immune system, it's because your heart is or has been feeling sad or you are holding onto emotions, thoughts and memories that are causing pain or sadness. This causes the heart to feel further cut off and disconnected from its Source and others.

The heart space can carry so much – despair, distrust, sadness, depression, fear, withdrawal, non-forgiveness, anger, disappointments, and grief. And it can carry so much goodness too – joy, bliss, love, compassion, healing, happiness, and a sense of ease.

We know how good we feel when things are completely aligned and we know how we feel when they are not. And often when they are not aligned it becomes

41

easy to blame the imbalance on others or things that were "done to us" or things that people didn't do. However, if we continue to point the fingers outward and deflect or project or protect, we are actually cutting ourselves off even further and separating ourselves from where our spirit is calling us.

Any change that occurs, any event that happens, any expectation that is unmet, any disappointment or pain are ways in which our higher self or Spirit is calling us out. It is calling us out on the things that are holding us back, asking us to let them go because they are only causing us pain and suffering. It calls us to step forward into a more open space where we can be free and fully aligned with the higher will of our being.

Every "test" (that's what many have come to believe they are… again, just a belief) is not actually a test, but rather a reflection of contrast to show us where we are, where we've been and where we can go to! The pain or conflict is there to show us the contrast between where we are, where we want to be and what we actually want in and for our life. When we begin to pay attention to the contrast as a teacher, we remember that we have choice – we can stay exactly where we are (in pain and suffering) or we can expand and take a step toward what we want and where we want to be. The choice is always ours to make and take. We can hold ourselves back in limitation and suffering, or we can let go and begin to trust that our higher self knows exactly where it is taking us by nudging us or showing us the possibilities of where we CAN go - to safer, more beautiful shores of expanded love and sense of self!

Pain is only ever the feeling that results when we are resisting where our soul wants us to go next. And your soul is always guiding you into expansion! Expansion! Expansion! Into feeling-better-spaces! We only need to let go of what we are or have been holding onto.

Natasha's Healing Story:

I had the pleasure of working with Natasha over a year, after she returned to Canada from being in the army in Israel. So much had shifted for her – change of country, relationship of the heart ending, saying goodbye to old friends, starting a completely different career path, and stepping into a world of new, with many questions, many concerns, many uncertainties and many decisions to be made. Her journey inward and back out again has been one that has deeply touched my heart – she has inspired me!

Here are the words she has shared with me: "Knowing that there is a person like Tara in my life is like having a constant safety net. I know that when things get blurry and I lose my intention or focus or whatever, I have her to go to, to help make sense of the life that I know that I want for myself. We are so lucky to live in an age where people like Tara use their gifts so openly and generously. Since seeing Tara I have gotten to love who I am on such a different level than I did before. I'm more proud and confident of who I am and of the path that I am on. Everyone I know who has gone to see her, comes back with extraordinary moment-altering results, and would all agree that her gift is one that teaches us how to re-direct our energy into love, alignment and bliss, which is what we all really want anyways."

Natasha Stern

Actress

Create space and freedom by releasing the attachments of this life.

We get so attached so easily to everything – our body, places, people, relationships, etc. If we can learn to just let go, even a little, and trust our connection to Source, we will always be led to greater and more fulfilling spaces and places! Sometimes we need to let go of the old to make room for the new… this includes old grief, old sadness, old painful memories, old ways of being, old hurt, old disappointments and old barriers that are begging to fall anyways.

For me, this time around my healing journey, I became aware that I was holding onto past pains, outdated ideals or thoughts around who certain people should be to me, and old filters that were causing me to see certain loved ones as not love and therefore more disappointment. I was definitely not seeing through the eyes of love or the heart. I was sitting in bitter resentment and emotionally-locked-off-protective-pain. It was time to let go and surrender back to the natural essence of my being. It was time to return to love and let it in once again.

How did I get there? I made a choice in my heart, in my body and in my mind that it was "time to let go" and free myself. I felt something inside of me shift. I felt a weight being lifted, the heaviness in my heart was releasing. I felt like I could breathe once again. I had no idea where this letting go would take me, however, I knew that anywhere was better than where I currently was. I was willing to trust and let go….

I found myself flowing into a very easy space of peace and clarity, as though my heart was guiding me back to where it always was. I felt open, relaxed and at ease for the first time in a while. I felt ready to release everything. I felt ready to open again and return to the Source energy that is me! I felt ready to emerge and surge and live and thrive! I felt complete with the process of things and of healing. I felt ready to stand, walk and live in the full awareness of my being! I felt ready to step into a way of being that is joyful and radiant and loving and filled with perfect health and wellbeing! I am ready! I am ready! I am ready!

I'm ready to walk with my HEART in my hand.

I was ready to accept my heart space as my best friend and I wanted only the very best for this friend. I felt as though it could and would lead me through anything and I was willing to trust its guidance as it held my hand.

And as I entered into this phase, I was sitting on the boat, listening to nature, taking in the goodness all around me… and the wind stirred! Indicating times of change… stirring it up, changing directions, purifying the last of my limiting thoughts and behaviours and patterns. Gathering them up and releasing them once and for all! Interestingly, wind or air is the element of the heart chakra – everything was finally in alignment and I could feel my heart singing with the wind.

I stepped outside to just stand in the wind and I uttered the words of release. I asked the wind to carrying away anything that was remaining that was holding me back. Sweep it away. Carry it back to Source. I choose freedom! I jump into a very new reality in which love and clarity are always present! In which I live and feel and think joyfully and am grateful for all the gifts that life presents to me! I am complete with pain and sifting! I choose clarity and joy and peace!

As I felt the energy shift, something jumped in the water in front of me, verifying or indicating that I had indeed jumped in! Jumped into the land of pure spirit and awakened living! I am awake! I am alive! I am here to thrive!!!!

On the return to healing the heart I felt love come alive within again. And with the help of the wind, I felt calm and assured that I could rest in trust and let the wind take me back to Source, knowing that all was well as I ride the waves of the wind current!

The following day I arose early, filled with an excitement toward life again. I did my yoga practice on the water, listening to nature all around me, taking in the breath of life. I felt a perfect sense of balance and harmony. I felt refilled and renewed. I felt strong, alive and wanted to share this love with the world. I wanted to speak only words of love. I wanted to share only vibrations of love. I wanted to expand it out to the world!

There are many things we can do in this phase to keep the heart open and expanded! Some of my favourites: (there are many :)

- ❖ **Loving another.** *Yes, simply just loving another and being present to the love that is in him or her will open and expand your heart!*

- ❖ **Choosing to see, feel and experience love in every moment of the day!** *This brings us into the present moment, which the heart loves, and we get to appreciate love and beauty all around us.*

- ❖ **Spend time with a pet and just love them all up.** *They are pure, unconditional love and can create such a joyful state within us! They light up our world.*

- ❖ **Get out, in nature.** *Nature is a natural rebalancer and heart-opener. We simply feel good when we're outside because we are connecting to all that is, including our breath and ability to slow down... pacing the heart to its natural rhythm.*

- ❖ **Hug someone!** *Hugs are healing in and of themselves! I LOVE hugs! And I mean a REAL hug...full on bear hug! I encourage you to Give & Receive at least 10 hugs a day!!!! I guarantee you will FEEL better!*

- ❖ **Eat and drink your love.** *Everything you eat or drink, imagine it as liquid love pouring into your body! Let yourself be filled up!*

- ❖ **Loving in Your Living.** *Do something loving for self, create a self-love practice and/or go out and pamper yourself! Or let every action, word and step be in/with a loving manner, way or intention.*

- ❖ **Flower Power.** *Buy some flowers that make your heart and face glow! The colours have a positive impact on your body too (colour therapy)!*

- ❖ **Musical Inspiration.** *Listen to some fun and playful music that generates a feeling of goodness. Something that inspires you, something that pulls* *on your own HEART-strings. Let it move you... like you want to sing and dance!*

* **Rest and Restore.** *Restorative yoga, postures that are heart opening and shivasana are beautiful practices that create the stillness that the heart needs to just melt, be and receive.*

* **Sing your way "home".** *Chanting or singing automatically opens the heart space because the heart is connected to the lungs and is the element of air. It's like pumping the heart by filling the lungs with the breath of life. It feels amazing when we open and let the breath pass over our vocal cords to sing the song that flows through us and from our heart! Try it! Even five minutes.*

All of this took me back to the simple act of saying one loving thing to another person. Looking a person in the eyes and saying something that is loving and compassionate from the openness of the heart! I had returned home once again... home to the fullness of my heart.

Your Heart's song...

If we can learn to live from the heart and listen to and with the heart, life would unfold much more gracefully! In the open, loving heart nothing is wrong. There is nothing to fix. There is nothing broken. There is nothing to heal because all is perfect as it is. All is in flow with the open channel of Source and the heart. All of our cells line up with this eternal love and our systems begin functioning at their optimum, including the immune system and our skin – you will literally GLOW! When we live from the heart life feels expanded and beautiful and so many loving gifts are presented! When we make decisions from the heart, we are actioning from a very whole and complete space – balanced in our masculine and feminine, our upper and lower awareness, our intuitive and intellect!

HEALING PRACTICE: "The Art of the Heart!"

Take some time to tune into your heart and as you breathe into this open heart space, ask your heart to show you love, to help you feel love, to expand love in all its forms. Ask it to utter its poetry, its art, its expression, and its song to you. It has so much to say! The heart knows truth. It has a direct line of communication to Spirit or Source.

I LOVE this topic and area of our experience so much! So much so, that I created a book all about love and my "love" story. This book, "The Love Manual - Learning to Live Life with an Open Heart", goes into great detail about how to live life from an open heart, how to clear the cobwebs of the heart, and how to access deeper love within so that your life is lit up!

When our heart is happy, it sings! It sends out energetic impulses to our body and out into our energy field! This vibrational song attunes or retunes our cells and our energy bodies to higher frequency – one that is aligned with the highest love, compassion and unconditional acceptance.

Every cell in your body comes to life with pure light and life force energy! Your channels open wide, your connection to the Divine strengths, you see, hear and feel more clearly and people all around you can feel the shift into love! They will want to be around you! They will want to be in your presence because you are vibrating from the heart and from love – the place that all of us innately know and want to return to!

When our heart is open and expanding fluidly, everything else feels, seems and looks better! Life seems more full! Love feels more loving! Things just seem easy! And the rest of the healing process is taken care of! We see things more clearly. We feel more clearly. We have access and openness to higher insights and knowing that all is well in the world and we know and feel that we are on the up and up and will and can move through anything! We know that we have so much support all around us and that love is present in everything.

Healing becomes easy when we are in an open, flowing heart space! We actually feel better because our immune system strengthens! Our thymus gland is connected to the heart and the thymus is responsible for our overall immune functioning. When your heart feels good, open and happy, you glow in so many ways! Your skin glows with vibrancy! Your immune system functions at its optimum! All systems are online and functioning in harmony with each other! There is no dis-ease. There is no imbalance. There is no friction or resistance. There is only openness and love! And an openness to give and receive and be a part of love!

Our intimacy with the people in our lives and to self increases and deepens. We begin to see them, self and the world from the eyes of pure unconditional love! We begin to live life in an entirely new way! We trust and know that the universe is working with and for us, not against... and we then trust that EVERYTHING that occurs or happens is not to us, but rather for us! For our continued expansion into more and deeper love! We remember why we came here and that we did it for love! We did it for the play! We did it for the sheer experience of expansion of life itself! Isn't it amazing when we can dance and play and set ourselves free!?! This is the ultimate heart-opening, the grandest expression of our heart!

HEALING PRACTICE: "Open Willingness."

The following questions have been created to open the doors of the heart by gently massaging it... When we are willing question where we are, we get to see our hang-ups, our blocks and where we're holding back. We also have the chance to see and feel where we want to go and possible ways to get there!

Are you willing to open your heart to the healing powers it has to offer?

Are you ready to release the protective layers that are no longer serving you?

Are you open to living a new way, overflowing with love?

If you've said YES to any of these questions, congratulations and a BIG YAY! You are ready to open to the next heart level!

HEALING PRACTICE: "Choosing LOVE!"

Take a moment to close your eyes and go within your body and mind and consciously choose to:

❖ Release anything that is holding you back. You know…the stuff that constricts your heart and ability to love. Take a deep breath and exhale it out of your body.

❖ Let go of the protective layers of the past that have you confined or in fear. Take a deep breath and exhale it out of your body.

❖ Breathe in the willingness to open your heart and live from an open space. Take a deep breath in and circulate it through your entire body. See this new breath moving through every part of you, bringing in new love.

❖ Breathe in and choose to live in love, harmony, balance, compassion, perfect health and wellbeing and joy. Take another deep breath in and circulate these through your body… trusting that every cell in your body is receiving the goodness that you are choosing for your new life!

And now take a few moments to just rest in the openness of your heart and feel the love circulating through you!

Once you open your eyes, write down three powerful LOVE statements that reflect how you are going to love yourself and the world more! Post them up for you to see regularly and repeat them to yourself often! Each time you do this you reconnect to the truth and the song of you heart!

LOVE is just like breathing...

Remember, the heart naturally knows LOVE! In the moments when you feel constriction or fear or not worthy of love, you are holding back from or cutting off where the heart wants to go. The other areas of your body and being respond because they are all connected to the physical and energetic heart and begin to close down also. Which can lead to self doubt in other areas (your gifts, ideas, etc.) and feelings of disconnection or unhappiness in general.

I've noticed in my own life, when I close off from love I immediately get sick. My body responds because love is not flowing and is being replaced by fear, judgment or anger. And then the external areas of my life close down or stop flowing. It's like my business and creativity shrinks. And if the gateway to creating heaven or bliss on earth is through the heart – which is love, compassion, openness, healing, joy, acceptance, giving and receiving – when we cut ourselves off from love on any level, if we constrict we are literally contracting our own energy field and contracting who we really are. And then we start to experience a small and limiting space and everything is effected by that. When we are in an open, loving space and we allow ourselves to go back into the flow and openness of our heart and lungs everything in our life, which is connected to US, starts to flourish as well and we start to feel better… like we can "breathe" again and we "glow". And you can return to love by choosing a loving thought and forget the rest… even if just for that moment. Let me just love for a moment.

And remember to BREATHE. Your heart chakra is connected to your lungs and your physical heart. When you lungs expand, your heart naturally expands also. When you take long, deep breaths the physical heart receives a burst of energy and vital life force. Which in turns expands to your energetic heart and allows it to "breathe" and open! The feeling or experience of LOVE is just like breathing… you allow the energy flow to in and out like a current and let your body do the rest as it receives and refills, and exhales the hang-ups and stagnant air. And in the moments when you feel as though you can't even take a deep breath in, still breathe, however focus your attention on the exhale and REAL-LY feel your body relax and soften as you exhale and release. Sometimes, in order to receive we need to let go, relax and soften… when we soften, we melt, which by default melts any constriction in and around the heart space. This creates an easy passage way for new energy, new love, new breath to enter in!

New Healing Habits for Heart Opening:

1. *Healing is easy when love is present! Just like a mom kissing a bump on her child's body, it's the love and compassion that allows the pain to wash away. That is the healing power we all have – LOVE! Choose LOVE!*

2. *Your heart knows love. It was built to love. It is meant to be open and flowing, just like the blood that pumps through it delivering to every cell in the body. All you have to do is give it the room to breathe and be open by allowing your self (thoughts, body, emotions, mind, ability to give and receive, ability to share and show compassion) to remain open. Make a choice right now to be open. There is nothing to fear.*

3. *When you are willing to live your life with an open heart, when you are grateful for all that has occurred in your life, the entire world will open to you! You literally will send out impulses or signals from your heart out into the world around that says, "I'm open. I'm loving. I'm love. I'm compassion. I respect this life that I have chosen to experience. I respect all other beings for their life. I care. I choose freedom." The energy in the world responds by sending to you more experiences to love and be grateful for!*

I LOVE YOU!!!!

CHAPTER 5

LISTEN TO
YOUR LANGUAGE

Your body and words speak Truth.

We often say things and just let them slide, with little awareness as to what we're really saying. Those little sayings are often an indication as to what's going on under the surface ("I've been too much in my head"; "I feel filled to the brim"; "I'm up to here and can't take any more in"; "I feel full"; "I can't say a thing"; "This is making me sick"; "I feel like I'm going to have a heart attack"). That's you speaking your truth. And sometimes our truth doesn't sound so nice or look so pretty. However, in that moment that is your body-mind truth and it's bubbling up to the surface to be released.

Keeping in mind that your "truth" can change in an instant. This may be the current truth statement that is simply based in your current knowing, which is often connected to your past. And this past isn't who you are any longer. So why do we hold on to a past that old, outdated and no longer true? Because we go on what we know and what's familiar… until that familiar way of being no longer works for us. We then have the greatest opportunity to listen and grow beyond where we currently are. We can choose a new belief system or thought patterning in any moment. And when we consistently choose this new pattern it becomes our new truth.

This gives a new meaning to the concept of truth then doesn't it? Truth is subjective to each person, based on his/her experience and his/her interpretation of that experience. And truth can change when we change. For example, at one time people fully believed that the earth was flat – that was their truth at that time based on what they knew. Now, our agreed upon truth is that the world is round. The same is true for one person looking at his/her life as struggle, pain, suffering, and everything goes wrong while another person who may be going through the exact same situational things may see his/her life as an opportunity for growth and loves how it has drawn up strength and courage within. Neither of these views are wrong… they are just different truths based on what each person believes to be true. And again, those truths can change… .

We all also have varying levels of truths – there is the higher truth which flows in from our expanded self and there is the lower truth which pushes its way in from our ego self. The ego truth is again based in the past, pain, hurt, protection, limitation, fear and its intention is for you to stay exactly where you are, to never grow beyond where you currently are. If we pay attention to this "truth" (I like to call it a false truth) we may notice feelings that are heavy, low, not supportive and more judgmental. Is this how you want to live? Is this how you want to feel? Are these the thoughts of truth you want to be communicating to yourself? What we feel, what we believe, what we think, what our "truths" are, are all being communicated out into the world, manifesting as our experiences. ALL OF THEM. That's how much power we have when we speak truth or whatever version of truth we choose in any moment.

Take a moment and look at what you see around you. What is showing up in your life, in your body, in your experiences? Now, what are the "truths" you hear, think, gravitate toward, feel or express on day-to-day basis? Can you see the correlation?

You do not have to be subject to this. You can experience a different version of life by changing your level of communication – this includes your thoughts, your comments, your words, and your beliefs. What you believe to be true is true. And that "truth" gets translated and sent out to the world or universe around you for instant manifestation. Want to change your reality? Change your "truths" and allow your communication to be more in alignment with the higher mind – higher self – higher communication.

This Higher communication is always happening within us. It exists within us. It is us. The only difference between those who can hear it and those who cannot is choice and awareness. The more mindful we become of our inner communication we can hear which level we are listening and speaking to.

Pause for a moment, take a few deep breaths and allow you exhale to soften you. As you inhale feel your body expand. Set the intention to open to listen to your higher voice. Imagine a larger sphere of light above your head and just focus on the expansion of it. See light streaming down to you. Let it fill you up just like the breath that you're breathing. "Show me my higher truth. Show me my higher voice." And then just rest, be still, receive and listen. You will begin to hear thoughts that are loving, nurturing, supportive, honouring, expanding. Just receive...... This is your higher voice communicating to you a higher truth about YOU and who YOU REALLY ARE. Now, notice how you feel?

Higher truth always brings forward a joyful, peaceful feeling within. Like everything is alright. Now knowing for yourself the difference between the two...... what truth do you choose for yourself? What voice do you want to listen to? What version of truth do you choose for your life?

As you continue to choose (it usually is a practice at first until this choice becomes as natural as breathing and becomes your natural state of being) you will begin to see or witness changes in your external world. Your experiences will begin to match the internal world, truth and communication that you have chosen! This is when life gets really fun, expanded and joyful!

You can choose speak words that reflect a higher truth or a lower truth. A higher truth surpasses the lack and limitations and ailments of this world and trusts that is it all for a higher learning, expansion, experience and growth. From this perspective we often lift right out of the density or pain and experience freedom. A lower truth would keep us stuck in the past, in pain, in blame, in suffering, and feeling out of control, helpless and like we are stuck in this forever. The choice is always ours / yours to make.

HEALING PRACTICE:
"Speaking from the Higher Voice"

For one week, choose the higher voice or higher truth of any experience. When the mind wants to confine or limit you to the past or to pain and suffering, use the power within you to step out of this lower truth, lift your voice and thoughts to a higher place that will love and support you, and allow a conscious-mindful truth arise within you. And then watch the effects of this on your health, wellbeing and life. If you feel good, I suggest extending this practice for another week. And if you feel good after this time, extend it for another week.... And if you feel soooooo good make it a choice for a month! It takes 30 days to introduce a new pattern or behavior and if you extend it to 60 days you're now anchoring it into your consciousness and by 90 days, you've fully established a new belief, pattern and automatic behavior! Imagine all that you will experience and create on a higher level during this time?!! WOW!

Bottling it only creates pressure within. And like any pressure cooker, it will pop if we don't lift the lid and let out the steam.

So many of us bottle and bottle and bottle and keep it all inside. Many are afraid to speak or admit such horrible thoughts or emotional outbursts. I'm here to say, it's okay! We all have thoughts that aren't so loving and happy and harmonious. And there was a long time that I denied myself the free expression of what was really there for me. And I completely understand why so many of us don't speak our true feelings when stuff is arising... often we have judged or criticized for feeling this way... often being seen in a negative light... and many times people don't know what to do when someone expresses in this way.

I would highly encourage everyone to be easy on the people around you and not judge or take personally what is being expressed. When someone is letting it go, your only "job" is to hold space and remember to bring your heart into it and see through the eyes of compassion. You don't "have" to say anything or do anything... and remember... please remember... the stuff they are sharing isn't truth, isn't a reflection of who they really are, isn't personal to you or anyone they are sharing about, and it really is just a moment of expression. When someone feels this type of space being held and created for them healing can actually occur because the pain expression has room and space to lift up and be released completely. The only way the "stuff" sticks around is when we attach ourselves to it...usually through judgment, un-comfortableness or fear.

When you admit and come clean with how you're feeling you create a release within that is so profound – you are no longer hiding, denying, defending or pretending. You are now speaking what needs to be spoken free from fear or shame.

Now, saying that, there are some things to take into consideration. When you are ready to express and get it all out, be sure to find a safe space to do that. There are many wonderfully gifted and loving practitioners out there who can hold compassionate space for you and will accept you in all of it – they know that you are not your pain and pain expression... they know that you are simply just expressing or emoting and that you are so much more. They can see your higher self and can help you to remember once again as well. And sometimes we need to "train" the people in our life so that they can better know how to hold space for us in situations like this.

Better out than in. When we store this stuff, it builds and gets stored and churns and turns into liquid tar which clogs our system on every level.

Here are some safe ways to express what you're moving through:

❖ *A journal is a great way to release, rant and purge. Write everything down, every thought, every emotion, and everything that comes into the field. And then when you're complete, rip the pages out and either tear them up and throw them out or burn the pages. You don't need to see or read them again – what's out is out and let it be gone and done.*

❖ *Going to or seeing a practitioner in the wellness field is another great option. He/she acts as a medium, who can simply listen, be a neutral support, lovingly see you clearly, hold compassionate space for you to do what you need, and then help you see clarity as you release it all.*

❖ *Retreating to nature is a beautiful option. It always embraces you and if you have the space to be alone in nature, you can talk or shout it out as much as you want! The elements of nature will absorb and recycle the toxic energy of what is being emoted.*

❖ *Talk to yourself or scream out loud by yourself. The key is getting IT out. You do not want those toxic thoughts and emotions to sit in you too long.*

❖ *Ask for what you need. Sometimes you may find yourself expressing or sharing to a friend or someone close to you just by habit or default. When we feel safe around certain people we feel it is safe to express. I would suggest taking one step before letting it rip... ask them for what you need from them*

❖ *Do you need him/her to just listen? Do you need him/her to just hold loving space for you? Do you want him/her to see you as the highest version of you possible? Or maybe it's all of this. Lovingly ask and let this person give to you so that you can shift and heal as you express.*

Most people are very sensitive and if we begin venting or lashing out without a second thought, with friends or even to our partners (whom are often the source of our frustration) if effects them. We often take advantage of this person by just spewing out without warning. The stuff coming up and out of you isn't really even about anyone else. It is your own stuff about your own stuff. The people are simply the catalysts or triggers. Please do not lash out at or on anyone. Most people receiving it take it personally, or it can create a domino effect that triggers him or her into their stuff and on and on we go and the cycle never ends. If we take a conscious step toward letting this person know what is happening and what we need while expressing it can dissolve the domino-downer effect and can create massive healing and awakened consciousness for both of you! Now we have conscious compassion communication!

Your VOICE has POWER.

The throat chakra (upper jaw) is the wheel of our power through our words, extended through the heart and down from our Source. It is the center of listening, communication, speaking our desires into reality and has a strong connection to your sacral chakra (lower jaw). Our throat power can either work for us or against us. When working for us we communicate words of love, possibility, appreciation and joy. We literally speak wellness into our body and experience. We receive direction from our thoughts and utter the words into reality! We help to create our reality through our words!

Take a moment to think about and feel into something you want to create your life… then utter them into form through your words….” Wouldn't it be (fun), (nice), (awesome) to _____

_____!”

And if you want to expand it even further, find someone who lovingly supports you (you can even email me! I love hearing from people on what they are creating in the world! tara@tarahealingsanctuary.com) and share with them what you're creating in the world! When you bring words to your thoughts you set them in motion for creation easy and quickly! You stand in your full creative power using ALL of YOU – your loving and joyful heart, your powerful solar plexus, your sacral creative energy, your grounded root, your 3rd eye sight for what you want, your crown chakra knowing that it is already done, and your throat speaks it into reality!

When our words (and thoughts) are working against us, we feel limited, we notice ourselves speaking words of negativity or judgment and we begin to see signs in our body that reflect this negative view and choice of words. We begin to see signs of this in our external world by how the world shows up. It is all in response to what we're sending out. The more you feel, think or speak anything, the more you'll see "proof" of it in your world – positive or negative, happy or sad, etc. This is the stuff we definitely want to shift so that we can live full out and create and be the fully expressive beings that we are! And create the world we WANT to live in and experience! We are infinitely creative by nature! Time to speak UP (higher speaking and truth).

HEALING PRACTICE:
"Reflecting on our words."

Use the following space to write down your thoughts and answers to the following questions. Begin to reflect on and notice the quality of your words.

❖ What are you saying to yourself and to others, in your written words, in emails, on Facebook posts, etc? Write down some common things/phrases/complaints you say or write.

_____

_____

_____

_____

_____

Do you feel good in saying these things?

_____

_____

_____

❖ Do you feel elevated or depressed? Happy or angry? (in these words/expressions)

_____

_____

_____

❖ What is the response of the people receiving your words? How do people feel or react in hearing or reading your words? (supportive, sad, shy away, withdrawn, uplifted, bright, etc.)

_____

_____

_____

_____

_____

HEALING PRACTICE:
"The Ultimate Throat Lozenge."

When you decide to heal at the throat level many options are available to you.

❖ Make a conscious choice to only say loving words to people and self for 10 days and observe what happens....

❖ Listen to music that is uplifting with positive messages. Music has such an effect on our body and vibration – lifting or lowering it depending on what we take in through our ears, which translates onto our nerve cells and affects the rest of the body. We can increase our blood flow or calm it down depending on the external that we are listening to. This is a GREAT option for anyone who lives in a toxic environment with a lot of yelling, arguing or fighting. You can always choose what you tune into. The more you "tune-up" or "re-tune" what you're listening to you will transform and the life around you will reflect what you're taking in and embodying!

❖ Listen to inspirational teachings or audio programs. The more you take in the positive stuff, you literally reprogram and move out the negative voices. Repetition is key to total transformation! What you hear over and over and over again will have an effect on you – one way or the other.

❖ And if there ever comes a time when you can't find the words, chant it out or sing to your heart's content! Singing, making vocal sounds or chanting are fantastic ways to clearing the build up energy trying to finds its way out!!!! "Shout, shout, let it all out! These are the things I can do without. Come on. It's happening to you. Come on."

I love singing. When I was younger and going through an emotionally turbulent time I naturally found myself in my room, by myself, singing for hours. I didn't vent to anyone, I didn't lash out on anyone. I simply retreated and sang and sang and sang! The energy that released was fantastic! I felt amazing, elated and back in my centered peace for days and weeks afterward! Try it out!

Communicate with and from the Heart.

There are and will be times when you'll want to communicate with loved ones or find yourself sharing things that you've gone through. We do this naturally as a community. It's one of the ways we teach one another – through sharing our experiences. To give someone another perspective on life and to let others know that they are not alone… we all go through stuff. It's a way of connecting or relating to one another.

Once we've healed the energy around the throat we can begin to communicate with more clarity. At this stage of sharing, the emotional charge is complete and gone and you can share from a higher perspective and point of view instead of the drama filled space that you may have been in when you were going through the painful clearing process or release. This is also the point that we communicate from the clarity and compassion of the heart rather than the reactive energy of your emotions or triggers.

And when the heart is open and flowing in harmony with our words we begin to communicate on an entirely new level. Many people still primarily use their intellect or rational mind to communicate – what would sound best, how can I get what I want, and I have to say things right or perfect. This becomes so programmed that the words almost seem empty or disconnected. The heart is missing from this way of communication and it becomes head focused rather than heart infused. When I go into a session or am about to speak in front of a group, I always say, "Higher self, I ask that you speak through me, teach through me and lead through me." I do this so that the lower voice in me is moved out of the way and my higher, expanded self and voice of the heart and soul can move through me and flow out. It makes speaking much more expanded, loving and enjoyable!!! And I get to experience the rush of Pure Life Force Energy! People feel the difference from this type of communication – it feels more authentic, more loving, and more supportive.

Brittany's Healing Story:

Brittany committed to changing and expanding her life in a BIG way. We did sessions together over a year and WOW....the transformation and expansion that occurred was remarkable and beautiful! Matters of the heart and relationship were the topic of healing during the first few sessions. Quickly the journey inward became the focus, where falling in love with self was essential, opening the heart again was necessary, and learning to speak with a clear and empowered voice with the higher self was vital. Throughout the year so much growth happened! It was amazing to witness Brittany's journey! She stepped into great places of power within, harnessed her emotions to become a more embodied actress, found her authentic voice, gained great clarity within her life, healed the hold-ups of her past, and is fully living the dreams of her higher-expanded self everyday!

Here's an email she sent to me one day after a phone session: "I just wanted to share some good news with you.....I found out yesterday that I booked the lead role in that film. !!!! It's so wild. This weekend, I worked through so much resistance. I realized so many things, one major thing in particular that had been blocking me repeatedly whenever I got close to getting something big. This is the first time in as long as I can remember that I have been able to do my best work when I've known I'm the top choice for a role. It's huge. Even though the weekend was so hard, and all of these obstacles were coming up in me, I was able to come back to this place of strength. There was always this part of me that knew I could rise above it, in a way I haven't been able to know before. For the first time, I didn't take the doubts or the habitual ways of negative thinking seriously, they had no merit anymore. They came and went, but I was always able to come back to the truth: that expressing the fullness of who I am - in my life and in my art - is good. Is nothing but good. It comes from goodness and is received as goodness. And finally, I feel myself knowing this. I thank you for this, Tara."

Brittany Allen,
Actress & Writer

Communication is key and is very important. And that includes communication with self, to self, with Source, and with others. Sometimes you may want to share, while other times you may find that not EVERYTHING needs to be shared or spoken to another. Words can be healing, neutral or destructive. Be mindful of which of these you are bringing forth when you choose to speak or share or communicate.

And maybe ask yourself, just in the moments before you utter the words, "Am I about to say words that heal or words that may be painful? Are my words coming from love or are they coming from hurt? How can I be more neutral or loving in my communication or choice of expression?" These simple questions of reflection will go a long way in improving your relationships and expanding your language of compassion and communication that is aligned with your higher self. And you will discover a whole new world of healthy communication, connection and compassion – within self and in your external relationships!

Here are a few other helper tools to strengthen or rebalance your throat chakra...

❖ **Wear or think or feel the colour blue.** *Blue light is very healing, cooling and has an opening effect. When the throat feels tight, imagine blue light passing through and opening your airways!*

❖ *The crystal lapis lazuli* has powerful healing properties. Place it around your neck or sleep with it under your pillow or carry it in your pocket.

❖ *Practice sharing your story or truth.* There are so many avenues to do this today – video, audio, radio, blogs, writing, person-to-person. We all have a story inside of us just waiting to be let out into the world! When we share we can actually shift the life of another. The greatest spiritual teachers in the world were storytellers! What's Your Story???? I would LOVE to hear about it! Feel free to send it to me!

New Healing Habits for a Higher Communication:

1. *Speaking your truth can change over time as change. What you believe to be true is true. You can choose to listen to and speak truth from your Higher Self or your lower self... the choice is always yours to make.*

2. *You can teach the people around you what you need and how to hold space for you when you simply need to vent or release. You could say something like this, "I love and appreciate you so much, and right now I simply just need to release and get this off my chest. I ask that you just love me through it, don't see me as something's wrong, and instead see me in my highest light so that I can move through this easily. Can you help me with this?" Now you have conscious compassion communication!*

3. *Bring your heart to your throat and speak only words of love and watch your life evolve around you to one of joyous compassion and abundant things to be grateful for!*

CHAPTER 6

CLEARING THE MIND, SEEING CLEARLY & FREEING YOUR BODY

Where are you right NOW?

We are all always connected to Source or Spirit or God or the Universal Life Force Energy. Always! The more we do this awareness work the more realize that WE ARE IT! We are the creators of our reality and life. Therefore, from this truth and knowing we don't need to spend hours or years trying to get "there". We already are "there" or here – already connected to Spirit, already embodying it, already healed, already whole and complete, already living the life we want.

Knowing this gives us a chance to breathe and let ourselves off the hook in the various areas of life or experience. In knowing that you are already, always connected to Source (that you are Source energy) all you have to do is just be there! Rest there! Feel into it! And remember that YOU ARE IT! Choose your NOW moment and where you'd like to be and IT IS DONE! Set aside time to commune with Source or your higher mind or just be with it all. It's really that simple. And when you do, the rush of life or life force will flow through you like waves of peace and stillness and love and pure knowing. It will fill you up and restore you to that place and space of perfection which YOU ARE!

Your NOW moment will become loving, peaceful, joyful, healthy, balanced, or whatever else it is that you desire.

HEALING PRACTICE:
"The Perfect Now."

Take a moment to notice where you are, what's around you, how you feel and what's happening. Get present. Let the other distractions of the mind melt away and be still in where you are right now. In the moment that you do this, you will feel a reconnection begin, a deep sense of calm and stillness will wash over you and pure Source energy will surge through you. As you breathe in, say to yourself, "All is well in the world. I am here. I am grounded. I am present. My now moment is perfect in what it is right now." Let all else fall away......

Use your Third-Eye & Mind to heal you.

The third-eye is such a powerful chakra! It is like a laser beam – focusing the energy of our thoughts and projecting them out into the world! It sees everything. It processes so much information. Think about your physical eyes – they take in so much information and stimulus without you having to think about what's going on. You just automatically know what to do and how to respond. The work is done for you! Now imagine that mechanism multiplied infinitely. This is the magnitude of your third eye! It is like a magic eye that is all-seeing. It is also the seat of your imagination and your intuitive knowing, where you process higher information and knowing and truth.

When the third-eye is open we can think clearly, we see clearly (literally and figuratively), we can accurately focus our intentions out into the world and we get to dream BIG into the realm of our imagination! Many wonderful ideas and creative projects are initialized in this chakra!

When the third-eye is closed or imbalanced we tend to see ourselves in a negative or limiting view and we see through a tight or closed lens. Our ability to generate new and innovative ideas is slowed or sluggish and we often experience headaches, eye strain or sinus issues.

Along my "healing" journey I learned many modalities and forms of healing. Some have fallen away over the years, some have changed, while others have remained a foundational part of the healing process or transformative journey! One of these modalities that I still use every day is – Source Connection Belief System Clearing.

It works so fast and clear! It helps to free the mind from plaguing thoughts, it cleans the emotions that feel like toxic waste and it releases the hold on and in the body, creating more space for light to travel inward! Every part of your being will breathe itself awake and to life! Every cell in your body will empty its toxic contents and open to refill with pure love and light, expanding the physical cells to receive more light and nourishment than ever before!

As we experience life, things happen, stuff comes up. We ride through the continuous wave of emotions, triggers, belief systems and thought patterns. So much is happening in every moment and often we life live completely unaware of what's happening or the effects on our entire system. Many of our belief systems are outdated, not allowing us to function at our highest capacity – even if we are spiritually growing and accelerating. It's like putting in a new high-speed program into your 1990 computer. It simply cannot integrate or assimilate the information or energetic light data. So, what do we need to do – change the hardware! Your belief systems are like hardware and your thoughts are the output from the functioning of the hardware. It's not simply a matter of changing your thoughts or lifting them to higher places. We MUST change the filters through which the thoughts travel through – these are your belief systems.

And we all have them! We have been picking them up since the day we were born. Absorbing the world around us in all its forms. Listening to the words and advice that is so loosely thrown around. Taking in other's beliefs as if they were our own. Over time they build up, stack up and create an entire form from which we live our life and perceive the world and act from. Some beliefs are beneficial to us and allow us to expand and grow, while others are limiting and create fear or separation.

Remember, the world is like a massive mirror, reflecting everything that we believe back unto us to experience, grow from and maybe one day make a different choice so that we can evolve past the current image.

Take a look around your life – what do you see? What shows up for you? What constantly comes into your experience?

As you observe, know that EVERYTHING that comes to you is NOT AT YOU but FOR YOU. For you to see clearly where you are vibrating at, where you are functioning from, where you are and where you can grow to. You DO NOT HAVE TO STAY WHERE YOU ARE! YOU CAN CHANGE YOUR LIFE BY CHANGING YOUR BELIEFS!

As you observe what is coming to you in your life, make note of it, write down what is happening and what you feel and what you see. As you do this you will begin to see repeating patterns, descriptions, phrases, and feelings. As you notice the patterns begin to sum up the descriptions as core beliefs.

For example, let's say you notice thoughts like:

"I'm not good enough."

"Life is hard."

"I'm never going to get anywhere."

You can see that these thoughts are definitely not directing you toward feeling positive. As you look a little deeper at it and peer through an expanded eye you may see a repeating pattern of lack, lack of trust, fear, resistance or unworthiness. These would represent core beliefs you have about yourself, life and the way the world functions. In that moment, you can choose to keep them if you like them or feel good about them. OR, you can choose to clean them up and shift them.

HEALING PRACTICE:
"Cleaning it UP."

When you're ready to shift and release and let go, find a quiet space where you can rest. Sit in a chair or on the floor, as long as your spine is upright. Close your eyes, rest your hands in your lap, feel grounded in your sitting and take a few deep breaths. Feel the stillness of your body and rhythm of your breath.

As you do this you are creating a peaceful space in your entire being. It is in this moment that you are returning or remembering Spirit or Source. You are remembering your connection and allowing it to expand to and through you.

As you begin to feel this connection in your body, begin to run through the list of beliefs and consciously choose to release, clear or let go of them. This is YOU, USING THE POWER OF YOUR MIND with YOUR CONSCIOUS WILL with the POWER OF PURE SOURCE ENERGY – ALL WORKING TOGETHER to create harmony and balance and restore you to your perfect nature of light!

It's not so much of what or how you say it, it's your intention behind the words. Set the intention for clearing – clearing your thoughts, clearing your belief systems, clearing your emotions and clearing your physical body! You are that powerful! Use what Source gave you :)

You may say something like, "I choose to clear all limiting belief systems that no longer serve me."

Or, "Spirit, help me clear all belief systems that limit me or create disharmony in my being."

Or, "Clearing all thoughts of anger, frustration, resentment and fear."

Choose to clear anything and everything that no longer serves you or has you feeling good. Choose to clear your belief systems, individual thoughts, old memories, old patterns, painful emotions, even things that you may have said or done that has you feeling guilty or shameful.

When I returned to this healing truth or modality, I was moving through a lot of "stuff" that I had been harboring in my body for two years… building up, accumulating and acquiring things that turned into full-on waste product in my body. Somewhere along the way I stopped listening, stopped paying attention to what my thoughts, emotions and body were telling me. So much so, that my body and face and head were screaming in welted pain and histamine swelling two to three times its normal size. I realized I was allergic to myself – to all the beliefs and pain that I was carrying around. It was time to release the pain of the past and all that came with it. It was time to reconnect and remember who I am and that I have all the power and wisdom within to recover from this and return to my natural state of balance and harmony and perfection.

And so, I began clearing one thought and emotion at a time – clearing all anger, fear, resentment, pain, guilt, shame, constriction, pissed off energy, all beliefs around men being not trustworthy, all beliefs around women being conniving and backstabbing, all beliefs that I had to save everyone. It all cleared. One moment at a time I felt the release in my body, I started to cry, yawn, burb and move in my body. Sounds started coming out of me that were so primal.

As you run through these clearings, expect the unexpected as to how the body wants to release – crying, yawning, burping, farting, stretching, shaking, body buzzing – all is game when we are clearing at such a cellular level. And be sure to drink lots of water to replenish and help the body flush any residual waste from your cells.

Let there BE LIGHT!

As you clean and clear your third eye, you will begin to "SEE" more light! Many people after a healing session or meditation literally describe the experience of opening their eyes as being able to see more light. As if the world around them is brighter. What has happened is you have cleared the cobwebs over your inner eye lens, you've expanded to see from your higher self and you actually can take in more light around you. This allows you to see more clearly, more openly, and more powerfully!

HEALING PRACTICE:
"Refilling the Well."

When you feel clear – more spacious, lifted, easy, light, elevated, happy, neutral – it is time to replenish, just like with water. Begin to refill and replenish with simple emotions or thoughts of love, laughter, happiness, gratefulness, joy, peace, acceptance, or grace.

You may want to say out loud or to yourself, "I breathe in pure love."

Or, "I open to receive pure light."

Or, "Source, fill me with love, joy, bliss and beauty!"

Say what feels good and light to you! You know your self, trust that the Divine will deliver to you! You simply need to set the intention and it will happen!

Breathe these things into your awareness and body. Feel Source delivering to you the most beautiful and glorious gifts! Let yourself be bathed in light and pure love straight from Source! And then just sit in it! Feel into it! Let your entire being remember what it's like to feel and be pure and whole and complete and perfectly aligned with Source!

Let your mind be the powerful conductor that it is! Let it bring in the highest vibrations of thoughts and emotions possible. Let it be a tool to reconnect you to Source and remember this connection every single day! The more you do this, the clearer you will remain! And the more filled up with Light you will be!!!!

Even NOW, as you read through these words your entire being is being tuned up and activated to receive the wisdom that is already there and present within you… simply awakening. Take a moment to just receive the words and energy that is flowing through to you NOW! Activating you, your cells and your innate healing wisdom!

Jessica's Healing Story:

"I first met Tara in the summer of 2008. She introduced herself and as we got to know one another, she expressed to me how she was an intuitive healer, amongst many other professions, dealing with healing and living a life of honesty and growth. Immediately, I was intrigued. Since I was a little girl, I always had detailed dreams and intuitions, which fueled my interest in healing, meditation, dream analysis, acupuncture, yoga, massage, energy work, and anything that had dealt with healing the mind, body, and spirit. When Tara said that she did sessions, I made an appointment right away.

I have had many sessions with Tara since meeting her. Life throws curve balls and I have been very blessed. Tara has helped guide me to have a more clear balance within myself, that greatly serves me with tools in how to deal with life and create my own reality. At times, I've been worried, stressed, letting my monkey mind take over and Tara's sessions have inspired me, as well have kept me balanced and present in life. Tara has an innate sense, understanding and knowing that blows my mind. Before sessions, I may have felt uneasy or anxious. During sessions, I am taken to a place of truth, my highest self, and knowing, and am forever grateful. After sessions, I am clear, relaxed, open, and feel way more grounded, connected to the universe, as well as to my higher self.

Tara has helped me connect to my truth and my skills as an intuitive. We all have the answers within us, but it can be difficult or overwhelming at times. Tara not only helps me see clear through specific situations, she helps remind me understand how I want to be, and how I want to live my life, creating my own reality. Whether I have something on my mind or am actually feeling great and balanced, I am always drawn to doing sessions with Tara.

In our first session together, I was brought to tears because she saw and knew things about my life that I never shared with her. She is able to tap into the spirit world, connect with people that have been in, or are currently in my life, guiding me to the present and not let my monkey mind get in the way. She has this quality of sensing what is best in the situation while doing a session. Most of the time, I am needing or wanting energy work, with a guided meditation to help clear anything that doesn't serve me. I sometimes fall into a deep sleep. What's really been beneficial for me is that Tara records our sessions (only her voice). I consistently listen to her to help remind me what we worked on, or help me meditate on a regular basis. My sleep is consistently inconsistent, as we process a lot in our dreams. When I am restless, I often listen to Tara's guided meditations or past recorded sessions to assist in dropping my metabolic rate so much, conducive to sleep, so I may get the rest I need, as well as have reassurance in how I want to live my life, creating my own reality.

I am forever grateful and will continue to utilize Tara as therapy for me to have a happy, full life, trusting my highest truth. I am truly blessed to have Tara in my life, not only as a guide, but as a dear friend. She has so much love and light to give, it is infectious. I only wish for everyone to have similar experiences I've had with Tara. She continues to serve and help me through my journey and I am forever thankful."

Jess Harper,

Dancer, Choreographer, Yoga Teacher, Los Angeles

Your imagination is the doorway – the gateway between your Higher Mind/Self and your intuition!

Let your imaginative mind take you a trip everyday! Day dreaming is one of the most powerful things we can do to create a new reality on any level! Just like when we were kids, we imagined all the time – what we'd become, what we'd do, the worlds we wanted to explore – we created worlds and experiences all of the time through our imagination. We were never bored by this. And the options were (and still are) endless. And the mind doesn't know the difference between what is real out there or what is real in here. It responds to both images or realities.

So if your external world, reality, body experience, relationships, etc. are not really where you want them to be begin imagining what YOU DO WANT TO SEE. Your subconscious mind will begin working with that imagine and will do what's necessary to create that an actual reality for you to experience. Athletes use visualization all of the time to enhance their skills and reach their goals. There are several studies that took three groups of athletes – one group who did nothing different and continued their regular regimen; the second did their regular workouts and regimen and visualized their body gaining strength or the game/outcome being favourable; and the third group did just visualization alone to see their body gaining strength or the game/outcome being favourable. Guess what happened???? The second and third groups had the best outcomes and surpassed the first group who was just doing physical work. And the third group that did just visualization gained the same strength as those working out and had the same game outcomes as the second group. The mind is extremely powerful!

I had this experience when I was doing a lot of yoga and working out and tore the tissue around my sternum. I actually heard a pop when it happened and then complete burning throughout my chest. For six months I couldn't do any plank postures, let alone workout without my chest ripping open again. I had to stop any physical activity that involved my upper body. I felt really sad because I fully enjoyed doing yoga and feeling strong physically. So, instead of sitting in paralysis I would put in my earphones and listen to my favourite music (sometimes yogic, sometimes workout/dance) and imagined doing my yoga practice or full-out dancing for 20 – 40 minutes! I felt amazing after! I actually could feel the muscle fibers in my body twitching and acting as though I was really doing it! And guess what happened? My body stayed in tip-top shape and my muscles stayed toned. I would also take five minutes to visualize the muscles in my sternum repairing and day-by-day I could feel the physical structure becoming healthier!

Whatever you want to see for yourself, your body, your life and your experience begin visualizing it! "SEE" every detail, how you feel while experiencing it and let your imaginative mind create with the same ease that you did as a child. As you do this, you strengthen the connection between your higher mind, your intuition and your body. They all begin to work together in harmony... and overflow result is happiness, joy, and experiences that we WANT TO HAVE!

And if you ever want a little extra help and support to "get there" guided meditations and visualizations are a wonderful tool! They help to refocus the mind and thoughts, guiding the inner eye to focus on visions that support and heal, while your body rests, receives, realigns, heals and rebalances.

This is the ultimate freeing of your body while refocusing the mind! Your body wants to be happy and healthy. Think of your thoughts and mind projections as food for your body. What are you feeding it? What do you want to feed it? Every time you use your imagination to create the world you want to see, you are feeding your body!

Seeing beyond your normal vision...

As you awaken and reignite the third eye you may feel impulses to create something new. You may have an expanded vision for your life! You may even have a burst in your intuitive abilities (a natural by-product of clearing this area). The world is your playground and your vision is your director of the show! Let's "see" what you can and will expand into!!!!

Other awakening tools for the third-eye:

❖ *Meditation & visualization combined is essential! This practice will offer you a new world to explore as you step outside your normal and into a dimension! There are many guided meditations out there – listen to ones that feel good to you!*

❖ *Painting and drawing are amazing tools to take what you see inside and bring them out into your external world to view! Plus it engages your throat, heart and sacral chakras as well!*

❖ *Watch movies or read books that are fantasy or imagination provoking! They will carry you into worlds beyond what we think we know here.*

❖ *Write. Writing offers a channel or medium for our intuitive mind to flow through... just start writing without filtering it. You'll be surprised by what you discover or see.*

New Healing Habits for Clearing the Mind:

1. *Your third eye is like a massive projector – reflecting your thoughts from your mind into the world just like a projector machine. It takes a small image within and blows it up and reflects it out onto a wall or screen so that you can fully see and experience the information there. What are you projecting into your world? What do you want to see?*

2. *You can heal your body by seeing the image within your mind and inner eye. Your vision isn't limited to what you "see" with your physical eyes... Your inner eye is a thousand, a million, a kajillion times stronger and more powerful than your two physical eyes put together! What you see inside will translate our into your physical reality!*

3. *You can expand and enhance your intuition by meditating, going within, paying attention to your thoughts and actively using your third eye to imagine anything and everything that you want! Your imagination is the doorway – the gateway between your Higher Mind/Self and your intuition!*

CHAPTER 7

OPEN YOUR HIGHER MIND

Last Resort – Last Stop – Your Mind

How do we heal when we've done all our inner work, have been creating consciously, have been mindful of our thoughts, have been communicating lovingly to ourselves and yet the body still screams while the mind is clear and the emotions are still?

IGNORE IT!

It's the ego's last attempt to hold you in confinement or in your body. Remember it does not want you to be free and when it realizes it doesn't have a place in your thoughts or emotions any longer, it may show up in the body. It makes its appearance by bringing to the surface physical pain, discomfort, symptoms or imbalances that are often "hard" to ignore.

Your best "tactic" here is to ignore it. As "hard" as it might seem to ignore pain. Do what you need to nutritionally and maybe even take a modern medicine approach to manage any pain, to allow the space to clear through this once and for all.

In this state the ego is like a child throwing a major temper tantrum and it WANTS your attention. Therefore, the best medicine is to ignore it. It will pass.

It will lose its power over you and eventually diminish and dissolve and the body will once again return to a perfect state of balance, realigning to the positive healing thoughts you have been holding and creating for your experience.

HEALING PRACTICE:
"Easy Ignoring."

In the meantime, while your ego is tripping out, play with any or all of the following:

❖ Do something fun, something playful, and something joyful to remain in a positive state of mind and happy emotional space. Keep the vibrations high and lifted.

❖ Reach out for support.

❖ Go for a massage or body work session that has you feeling good.

❖ Do something that brings a state of joy.

❖ Listen to music!

❖ Do something/anything to distract your mind long enough so that the Source that is you will take over and steer the ship for a while, while you recalibrate!

These will help you remember your Source and reconnect to that beautiful space of pure energy! As you continue to remain there nothing else can enter and the ego begins to fade and release the grip.

Where's your focus?

What you focus on will expand. However sometimes we are so overwhelmed by life and all that is happening around us we can't see what our mind is focusing on. A powerful indication as to whether your thoughts or focus or serving you or not is to pay attention to how you feel. Do you feel uplifted? Energized? Alive? Vibrant? If so, then the thoughts and focus you're having are in alignment with health, vitality, higher self, etc. If, however, you feel tired, overwhelmed, exhausted, low energy, confused or lack of luster, then your focus and thoughts have most likely been in a "negative" or not so serving direction.

When we are consistently tired, it's because our focus has been on things that are tiring around us – grief, death, change, perceived loss, illness, etc. And even though these "things" may be happening or have happened, because all of your energy is going there, there is little room for anything higher, loving or nurturing to come in. And then we feel even more separated and cut off and tired. We also can miss any good that is happening around us because the focus is elsewhere and we're being clouded by the illusion of pain or loss or "terrible" thing. There is always good pouring in for us, to elevate us and move us out of the pain that we're in. There is always something to grow from in any situation. We just need to refocus for a moment and all the positive, happy, healthy, growth, supportive energy will be there. YOU can shift your focus to something different or more positive and lift your energy up!

HEALING PRACTICE:
Shift Your Focus

Consider all the "terrible" things that are happening in the world or in the lives of those around you. And instead of seeing the thing as being horrible, say to yourself, "Perhaps I could see this from a different perspective. Let me see and know a different perspective from my higher mind." And then just receive. Perhaps the new view becomes so simple, like, "Hmmm… perhaps this is happening for greater awareness for the world." Or, "Maybe he needs to experience grief to know how to release emotion." Or, "Maybe she is learning forgiveness on a deep level." By focusing here, you can magnify supportive and loving energy for that person or the world and help in the COMPLETION OF IT, INSTEAD OF CONTRIBUTING TO THE CONTINUATION OF IT.

The more we practice shifting our focus with the easy things in life or things that are not directly happening in our life, we become stronger and faster at shifting our focus when it relates to us. You'll be able to shift your perspective or focus on a dime.

Rising emotions will ebb and flow…

When healing at this level of awareness and busting through the grips of the ego you may find yourself feeling angry towards the ego or the body. That's okay – actively or consciously direct it at the ego instead of the body. The body is just receiving direction and interpreting information. The ego is stirring things up because we have given it so much attention over our lifetime and all of sudden you are not. It gets upset and tries every attempt to disturb your center or peace. Don't let it take over or control you.

There are times when the emotions serve as a gateway or indicator as to what's going on deeper within us. And we can use them to heal and release. However, there are other times when the emotions have become so out of control that they feel to be running our life, or we have invested so much time and energy on the emotions that they too become our focus or normal state of being. This is not healthy either and we need to balance them out. I had a situation occur with a client where she had experienced so much death around her while she was expanding her empathic abilities that the emotions she was going through were amplified by the emotional states of the people around her. It became so overwhelming that she was an emotional wreck. She couldn't see the happiness that was all around her, she couldn't be happy for the good things that were coming her way, all she could feel was sadness, tiredness, heaviness, overwhelm and shut-down… except when she was working with clients (more on this later).

Sometimes we need to shift our focus out of the emotions and up to our thoughts, which seems counter-intuitive for some people. We are told to get out of our head and into our body, to pay attention to how we feel… and yes, this is true SOMETIMES. Other times our emotions are the very things that are keeping us trapped, stuck in pain. And the only way out is to refocus. By investing more energy into figuring out or looking at the emotions we only amplify those emotions and feel even more sad, more tired, more overwhelmed, more in pain. We lose energy because of the power of the emotions instead of gaining energy. Think about a time when you had a total cry-fest… sobbing… heart-wrenching cry. How did you feel after? Perhaps drained and tired. Like you needed a good sleep after. Why? Because you gave so much attention to the emotion that was releasing and this has an effect on the body. And again, crying is not a bad thing… sometimes we need a good cry, sometimes it allows us to release pent up energy and gives us the opportunity to feel deeply. However when we find ourselves crying and crying and crying…. At some point we need to shift and go UP. You can feel sad and keep your thoughts elevated at the same time while you're moving through the tears or sadness.

Somewhere along the way the mind has received a bad rap. We are told that we are too much in our head… and yes, that can be true also. What we are looking to do is find balance – homeostasis – which is a constantly changing thing. We can definitely use the mind to help us heal! By drawing the focus up into the mind – the conscious, loving, supportive mind – we can lift right out of the emotions which no longer need figuring out and back into health, well-being and peace. This is the ability to move into the conscious mind, not the monkey-mindless-mind, which has powerful effects and ripples on every other part of our experience and body and emotions. And as a result your emotional scale will reset and begin to lift up as it follows the flow of our thoughts. And your body will feel more healthy and balanced. When your mind-field expands, your entire energy field will expand which will allow in more light energy from the divine!

HEALING PRACTICE:
Lift Out of the Emotions

Take a moment and close your eyes. Notice how you feel and all that is there without over identifying to it. No figuring out or asking questions this time. As you breathe, begin to draw your breath upward toward your mind, toward your head or crown.

And I want you to use your thoughts or the higher part of your mind and say to yourself, "I am complete with this phase. I choose a different way. I choose clarity. I choose focus. I choose to balance out my emotions and my thoughts. I am complete with my emotions running themselves. My thoughts now dictate my emotions."

Now start thinking about how you want to feel. And it might start out as I don't want to feel sad, etc. Let those surface and give indication as to what you want. And start simple. I want to feel peaceful. I want to feel free. I want to feel happy. I want to feel grateful. I want to feel hopeful. I choose to feel balanced. I choose to feel alive and healthy. I choose to feel light. I choose to feel energized. I choose to feel inspired. I choose to live from the relationship of my higher self and every day I choose to allow my higher self and emotions move through me, live through me, speak through me and have a positive effect on my emotions. At this time I choose to go UP. I choose to lift my view and focus from where it has been to a higher place.

Now notice how you feel.

After running through this exercise with this particular client she commented on how good she felt and how easy that was. She also mentioned that she remembered feeling the same lightness while she was working with clients and teaching, but when she returned home or wasn't working she felt all that heavy emotion return as it was waiting for her. Why was that? Because while at work and being of service her mind was focused elsewhere – not on her pain, not on the heavy emotions. All of that was put aside and forgotten because her mind had something different to focus on. You were in your expanded self...which always feels great! However, when she returned home, back to life where the norm had become one of pain and suffering, she didn't have anything else to do or focus on and her energy sunk back down into the basic earth experience, and therefore the old "stuff" came rushing in to fill the gap. I recommended to her for a few weeks to have some fun, new, productive things, healthy distractions for when she finishes work. So that she can consciously refocus her mind even in her spare time. Or meditate every night so that she can internally refocus! Remember, what ever we focus on expands.......

And when you practice this regularly you will develop the ability to reset and refocus your thoughts, and therefore your emotions, even when you're around other people who are moving through sadness, grief or heaviness. Which can in turn help elevate the people around you.

While writing this book, I was going through something rather trying (mysterious and unexplainable flare-ups in the body) and was being given the opportunity to refocus while allowing the emotions to rise up. As I went deeper into the emotion of what was surfacing I felt abandonment from Source. This was the ego's attempt to disillusion me once again and cut me off or have me feel cut off from Source. As I cried and cried and surrendered into it, I felt a deep anger rise up toward the ego. I started shouting in my mind and body and out loud, "You have no power here any longer! You have no place here any longer! I am done with this game you are playing. Get out! Get out! Get out! I am done with you!" As I was kneeling on the ground, my head in my hands, tears streaming down my face, my spine curved toward the ceiling, I felt a massive energetic lift as if something was being pulled from me, taken out. I felt the ego detaching and losing its power. I felt a release, a point of power and surrender at the same time. I started to laugh. I felt strong and empowered. I felt like everything was going to be okay!

Later that night while in bed writing this piece, I felt its distant cry, like a hurt child pleading to come back in. Trying to bring my awareness back to the lump on my forehead. I repeated, "No. No. No. You are no longer welcome here. I am no longer playing that game. I am here to live in peace and harmony and balance. And it is time for my body to align with this also! My cells return to Source and their God-like state of perfection. Right NOW!"

I felt my skin release. I felt myself breathe a lot deeper. I felt my joy return. I knew in that moment that all was well in my body and the world again. This process of learning from pain was complete. I felt pure Source energy flood through me and my crown chakra blew wide open once again! I felt completely connected to my Source and I trusted in the divine flow of it ALL!

And why did this yelling and shouting work? Because I was consciously choosing what I wanted to feel, where I wanted my thoughts to be and therefore it was!

I was ready to begin my journey of freedom, love, truth, peace, perfect wellbeing and harmony on every level of existence! I was ready for my freedom!

My POSITIVE POWER statements got real CLEAR:

- *I am ready for my peace!*

- *I am ready to feel whole and complete and in perfect alignment with Source at ALL times and in ALL ways!*

- *I am ready! I am ready! I am ready!*

- *I open to receive this truth! I open to receive this truth! I open to receive this truth!*

❖ *I know that I am loved and supported in every way and I know that my cells return to their perfect pristine state every day!*

❖ *I know that I am love! I am Source! I am connected to that infinite state of peace at all times!*

❖ *I can now rest in this truth and clarity forever and live fully expressed and joyfully in all ways of this existence!*

Thank you body for your wisdom and teachings. Thank you spirit for guiding the ship and course. Thank you higher self for helping me remember my truth! Thank you "God" for always being here to love and support me! I am eternally grateful!

Learning from the experience and detaching from the "pain" can be a powerful new place of creation!

Many of us have been taught that the only way to learn or grow is through pain. I have been there. I learned a lot... and yet I found myself becoming attached or addicted to pain, almost expecting it to show up so that I could grow. The lens I had been seeing or perceiving through was one of analyzing pain and then feeling empowered that I had grown through this pain. And this would work for a certain time period and then the exact same "stuff" would show up again and again. It felt as though nothing had really changed or healed completely. I began asking the question to my higher self, "Is this truth? Or is there an easier way? Show me...." My Higher mind answered, "This is learned truth. It is what you've been taught. There is an easier way. You get to choose how you want to learn – from pain and suffering or from joy and contrast."

My life completely changed after that inner conversation! In the experience here we will learn certain things through all sorts of emotions and dynamics.

How we get to this learning is actually up to us! We can learn the quick and easy way, free from pain, get the learning and expansion and move on. Or we can learn from the pain that is showing up. Either way we are going to learn something. We have been taught to suffer, to feel bad, to believe that pain is normal and that we have to live with is, and that the body is failing us. Does this feel like a higher truth to you? Does this feel supportive and loving to you? If not, then lets begin releasing the binds of pain and create a new way to learn… we have been doing it this way for thousands and thousands of years. And I don't know about you… but I'm ready for a new way of doing things! A new way of freedom and inner peace that supports our expansion and growth, rather than our deterioration.

How do we detach from the pain paradigm? We create a new definition of what pain is and why is shows up. We begin by remembering that everything is an experience for our expansion and growth. The only time pain is ever really present is when we are resisting the direction that is calling us or resisting the learning that can come from change or the experience. When we deny ourselves the opportunity for growth we feel the contraction of energy and therefore feel uncomfortable or pain. Pain is like a by-product from not listening or paying attention to where our soul is calling or directing us. It is not something that is normal or just happens. It flares up as an attempt to get our attention. So, then, if we start paying attention to the subtle signals that occur all of the time we will continue to move in the direction of our greatest growth with ease, joy and feeling good.

Some common subtle signals to listen to:

* ❖ *Gut feelings….*
* ❖ *Feeling good in the direction of this or the tightness from going toward that.*
* ❖ *Feeling sluggish when around certain people or situations – this is not normal, your energy is depleting. Pay attention as to why….*
* ❖ *Does my body feel good when I eat this?…. If not, then stop eating it.*

❖ *Is this what I really want to do?... No, then don't do it, listen to what you really want and move in that direction. Then witness how you feel.*

I know that we are on this experiential path of remembering or awakening and sometimes the first stone on this path of awakening appears or shows up as PAIN. An attempt to get our attention and to pay attention to the choices we are making and the path we are walking down. If listen we get to "graduate" or move on to an expanded level of awareness which leads us to a place of choosing our thoughts, which shape our reality, which allows us to expand from different emotions instead of always pain. We were not meant to stay confined or bound to pain or learning from pain. It was merely an opening, a loud call for change or action, a BIG flashing sign of awareness. Pain was not meant to be the norm. Living a painful life is not the way of your Higher mind or self or Spirit. That is "truth" of the lower self, the ego mind. Therefore, anything that says your only way to grow is through pain is something this is being lead from a different place than the higher heart and mind.

One step at a time.... Free yourself by facing your pain... and move on!

When pain surfaces in your life, take the opportunity to grow through your pain instead of from it. Take time to listen to what the pain or discomfort is communicating to you. Ask it, "What are you teaching me? What am I to learn from this?" And listen. Thank the pain from coming and then make a choice to let it go. The pain is no longer needed and it is time to release it. Use your breath, as well as the other tools from this book. Make a conscious choice to be complete with this type of learning (that's all it really is). "I choose to learn through contrast or joy or anything else....I choose to be listen more to what my body and being are communicating to me. I choose to pay attention so that I can get the learning faster and grow beyond this current state. I choose to learn from a higher place."

As you make these subtle changes you will see and experience massive results that catapult your life into magnificence, freedom and perfect well-being. This is the natural state of your crown chakra – the gateway that connects you to the higher versions of self. From this perspective we see only expansion, love, support, higher wisdom and higher truth.

And when we expand up to a higher version of truth or knowing we discover an easy pathway or way to ascension… Why? Because there's nothing stopping or blocking us from "getting there"… We realized that WE ARE THERE! We are already perfect, whole, complete, amazing, magnificent, thriving, infinite, creative, powerful, healed, and alive!

A Note on Spiritual Bypass

I felt called to write about this concept of "Spiritual Bypass" – a term often used in the new age world. When I learned of this phrase it was used a thing you don't want to do… that somehow you were avoiding your emotions or thoughts or things that were coming up and were bypassing the learning. During this time of my evolution I was sooooo in my body… sooooo in my emotions… sooooo in analysis of everything… what's does it mean? why is this happening???… that that was my world. This actually kept me bound to that reality that I was focused on – pain. And it began to extend out into the world around where I'd find myself holding heavy opinions and judgments about the people that I would see "spiritually bypassing". However, the one common thing that I noticed about their state… they were all freakin' happy. And that bothered me even more because I was thinking, "I've been doing all this inner work and self reflection and you haven't done anything. And I'm still miserable and in pain and there you are over there… happy as could be. They're not doing their inner work, they're not focusing on themselves. But, they're happy. WTF."

I realized at that moment that something was off… I was missing something. Maybe there was something to this spiritual bypassing thing because I wanted to be happy.

Today, from the awareness I have now, I do feel it's about finding the balance and using all the tools we have available to us. And sometimes the body is doorway to greater awareness. Sometimes the emotions are the trigger to expansion. Sometimes the over thinking is the constriction that sets us free. The key is to listen, pay attention, allow, get the gift of learning and MOVE ON! Return to bliss! Return to your SPIRITUAL SELF and nature!

And now if someone looked at me and said, "Wow Tara, you're totally spiritually bypassing." I'd say, "Yes and isn't that a great thing! I choose now to be happy. I choose to bypass that I'm limited to or controlled by my physical body. I'm passing through the emotional "stuff" that we can sometimes feel controlled and crazed by. I'm bypassing the limiting thoughts that have me confined or in pain and stuck. And all of this is of the human experience, not of my higher self, which is what I came here to learn – full embodiment of my higher self in this earth body or reality. I'm going straight to my higher self. How can that be a bad thing?" It's not. Up is where we're all going! It doesn't mean I'm going to leave my physical body. However, while I'm here I'm going to access those higher dimensions, realities and truth and bring them into my every day earth experience! Because I can! And because I choose to! Which is totally awesome! And I might have things that brush up against me however those are simply opportunities for me to grow and expand again. GET THE GROWTH and then move on from it so that you can return to bliss. We did not come here to suffer.

Caroline's Healing Story:

Caroline came to me at time when great change was occurring in her life that seemed confusing and conflicting with what she knew as truth. She had made some decisions that were not in alignment with who she thought she was and yet something larger than her was calling her toward it. On one hand, her heart was being led in certain direction that was loving, expanded and beyond any joy she had ever experienced and would create the perception of chaos on the other hand. She felt conflicted about what to do and what decision to make.

Once she stepped out of the confusion of her head and back into her heart, she found a connection to her expanded self that was clearing guiding her direction toward listening to her heart. When she made the decision to say YES to this greater expansion, freedom and complete joy was the outcome! She had surpassed her pain and stepped onto a path of greater awareness and ultimately greater JOY! Here's what she had to say after our time together: "At a crucial, tipping point in my life, I have turned to Tara for help and guidance.

I had no idea what to expect, just a deep and profound recognition that I needed something, a "light" that neither friends, family nor myself could provide me with.

This couple of one-on-one sessions has been simply magical. Stuck in pain and sadness, conflict and constant noise - as I was going through life changing decisions and experience - , Tara has brought the necessary peace to my internal chaos, the unconditional and non-judgmental support to my story and desires, and the strength to envision a possible and happy future for myself but also all the ones surrounding me.

The experience was similar to living in a house with blinds always closed and suddenly opening them: the room gets filled with light and warmth in the inside; but more importantly, there is a different world outside…a new way of thinking, the possibility to envision a reality and a future bigger than self.

Now armed with this magical spark, I thought participating in Tara's 6 R's workshop would be a good continuity to my journey of healing and positive change. This was an amazing experience. Tara's techniques to re-invent one's life are tools that can be applied to anything in life that you want to change. The approach is very practical and at the same time focuses on introspection work to be totally centered and balanced with whom you really are and what you really want. I left the workshop with a clear path of what I wanted but also the certainty that

I was strong enough to navigate through any storms and still find my happy place. I now believe in gifts in life and magical power...Tara has done that for me in ways beyond Awesome."

Caroline F,
Toronto ON

HEALING PRACTICE:
"I am Powerful!"

Take a few moments to write down your own Positive Power statements... write them in the present tense, make them real for you, say it the way you want it to be!

And then repeat, repeat, repeat, repeat, repeat, repeat... got it? The key is repetition – to replace the old statements that you've been telling yourself for years and bring in new ones that empower you and support you!

My Positive Power Statements:

_____

_____

_____

_____

_____

The Magnificence of OUR Expansion UP.

The crown chakra is the divine entry-and-exit to Source – the expanded version of who we really are! It is the infinite flower unfolding ever upward, opening to receive the energy from Source and forever calling us to be more of who we really are!

In its expanded, open state we trust in the flow of the Divine. We believe in something higher than self. We feel in alignment with ALL and ALL that is happening in our experience. We know that the Universe is working with and for us!

If ever we feel disconnected, not trusting, find ourselves questioning everything, or feeling confusion or direction-less then our crown chakra has closed somewhat. Often times as a result of limiting beliefs that cause us to question, doubt, not trust and separate ourselves from our Source. It happens to everyone at some point along the journey to expanded awareness. It can manifest in the body as depression, hopelessness, despair, confusion or mindlessness. However, when you begin to cultivate a relationship with your Higher Self through your crown, you remember your infinite self and power and all that other "stuff" simply falls off or away. The only way it hangs around is because we are choosing to stay attached to it through our beliefs or conscious will. Release the attachment, even for 10 minutes through meditation, and you will re-establish a greater connection to a part of you that is so profound you will not want to go back to living the "other" way ever again! Clarity, health, well-being and freedom can and will be yours again!

Here are my favourite ways to reconnect and re-tune your crown chakra up:

- ❖ ***Prayer is so powerful!*** *Even if you don't know how, simply pray – ask, intend, or talk to whatever it is you believe in. There are many studies around the world that show the powerful effects of prayer, especially when we come together in unified prayer or thoughts of good intentions!*

❖ *Connect to communities that uplift and inspire!* There are many plac-es around the world that act as sanctuaries for people to come together and unite under one roof. These spaces are powerful in uplifting whole communities to a higher state! And something magical happens when we unite with other humans on this path – we are often reminded that we are not alone and that our fellow travelers can hold us when we are down. There are also many online community presences. One of my favourites are Agape International Spiritual Centre in Los Angeles and my husband and I will be live-streaming our up-coming Expanding Awareness Events hosted live in Toronto, Canada! Please email me for more information!

❖ **Get out-side of yourself.** *If you don't know what to believe in anymore, get outside. Nature has a way of holding us and returning us to clarity!*

❖ **Positive affirmations** – *create powerful statements that leave you feeling GREAT. And repeat them!*

❖ **Meditation!!!** *Again, my favourite. Why? Because you can do it anywhere, anytime, for any length of time and as many times as you wish!!! It creates the space to center, ground, and connect to your breath (life itself0 and re-attune up to whatever it is that exists out there. Once you connect, you get to just sit and receive the flow of pure spiritual energy!*

❖ **Be open to know Source for you!** *As you release everything you know or think you know, you are more open to receive the Divine in a new way that is uniquely your own experience of Source! How cool!!!!*

New Healing Habits for Opening the Mind:

1. *When the ego screams in a final attempt to keep you confined it is persistent like a temper tantrum. You have the power to ignore it. KNOW like you've never known before, that you are healthy, well and vibrant! Make a firm stand that this is your new reality! You have the power to grow from pain or not. The choice is always yours.*

2. *Your crown chakra is a powerful gateway to knowing your Higher Truth, Higher Self, Higher Mind and Infinite self! Make a commitment to build the most important relationship and connection of your life!*

3. *Meditation is a powerful tool to reconnect to who and what you REALLY are. Five to ten minutes will "get you there". Simplify your meditating by either focusing on your breath or listen to a guided meditation to refocus your mind. Before you know it, you'll be taking the trip of you LIFE! And if you want additional support, check out Love Ignites Light Meditation CD on iTunes by Tara Antler.*

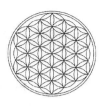

CHAPTER 8

BRINGING IT ALL TOGETHER & LIVING A HIGHER PATH!

Releasing the Definitions that Only Confine Us.

In letting go of ALL beliefs systems and returning to known truths, I had MANY belief systems regarding "healing" clear from my "truth bank", outdated systems that I had picked up over the years. One of these belief systems referred to "needing to go through pain and discomfort in order to heal or learn or grow". This is something we are taught. However, is it true? Do we NEED pain in order to grow? Does the process of expansion NEED to be painful and uncomfortable in order for us to reach heaven on earth? The answer that continued to surface time and time again was – NO. That was simply something that was taught to us over time and something to which the ego has clung and made real. Remember, the ego does not want harmony or peace. It only knows conflict, constriction and comfort.

Our higher mind or self knows only love, compassion, clarity and expansion, and it wants the same for all of us. It felt as though it were time for an upgrade in thinking and believing. This new truth, that poured through was this: We can CHOOSE to heal and grow and expand through JOY instead of pain. It is a conscious choice that EVERY being has say over!

In my own "process" of going through this release and expansion, I realized that my body continued to show signs of imbalance or disharmony or dysfunction. This was rather confusing to me. I was "doing" everything "right" – the right nutrients and herbs, the right thoughts, clear emotions, strong connection to Source and knowing that it was all that I needed to sustain and heal me. I was reaching out to other healers for assistance and clarity and I was meditating every day to feel my core and center. And yes, even through all of that clarity, ease and grace, my body – particularly my head and face – continued to swell with unknown welts and allergic reaction swelling three times normal physical appearance. I was perplexed. What was going here?

Use your body as a communication tool.

All of a sudden a line of questioning and insight began to flow to my awareness. The client I was seeing that day brought forward some questions to which I could answer so that I could hear truth once again!

"TRUTH! When there is resistance or a block to Source energy flow, we first let you know through your spirit body or layer. If you miss the message we funnel it down to your thought system and your thoughts start changing to reflect the imbalance or resistance. If you don't hear it then, we funnel it further down to your emotional body or layer and your feelings start to reflect the resistance – anger, rage, sadness, unplugged, disengaged, depressed, frustrated – sound familiar? And if you don't recognize the call for a shift we plow it down to the physical where you HAVE TO PAY ATTENTION! We have been saying all along, Pay attention! You are creating or causing resistance here. Time to shift and recalibrate."

For an entire year I practiced not giving the physical body welts and flare-ups any attention. I was not going to feed the ego-temper-tantrum any longer and so I carried on with the belief that everything was well and returned to its perfect health and wellbeing. However, in this aha moment, I recognized that

I was still missing a piece of the puzzle... a piece I had not yet looked at......
a major source of resistance within me that was calling for healing, elevation,
transformation and expansion.

In that moment, I remembered the truth – that the body is a communication
device or vehicle – always sending us signals of alignment or misalignment. I
just wasn't fully listening, or rather had gone to the extreme of ignoring while
the child still kicked and screamed in discomfort. It may have been a better
option to pay attention, communicate, find out the source of resistance, clear it,
realign and then ignore the remaining "symptoms" as they healed and cleared
completely from the physical and all reset itself with ease and grace.

So, this time, I took the time to listen. I slowed down, went into a meditative
space and quietly and gently asked my body to tell me what I was missing, what
was I ignoring, what was the initial resistance about? And ALL got still and
then clarity rushed in like a cleansing wave of water! I remembered or recalled
the initial resistance that was building inside of me like a volcano of unhealed
emotions... raging and lashing out inside and externally. It was time to "face"
the resistance, call it out, speak it and then make a choice to clear it once and for
all. I was time to reset the entire system! I was ready! I felt clear and brave and
strong! I could face this! And so it was! I revealed all that I was holding onto
and could now see the falseness of the resistance. It was time to release it and
let go from not only my body, but also my emotions, my thoughts and allow
pure Source energy to rush over me to bring me back into perfect alignment.

The healing was easy from this point forward! My body restored itself. No welts
or swelling showed up any longer. I felt strong and healthy and fully restored!
We worked as a collective team!!! My helpers in the physical and non-physical
and the empowerment of self helped deliver the wisdom that exists!

As I complete this paragraph, I was reminded of our family dog, Mya. A few
days prior to this awakening and release, she was eating grass all day. It was
strange because she did not seem sick or not well. And yet, she ate and ate and
ate and drank a ton of water. And then in hourly cycles she would help her

body throw up the partially digested grass along with bile and bits of other food. I couldn't believe how much she was releasing. And what amazed me even more was the innate knowing as to what to do to help relieve her discomfort or imbalance. She knew exactly what to do! And after 5 cycles of this, she was perfect and back to her normal happy, relaxed and well self! She did not need my help, she simply retreated to her inner knowing and trusted her body to tell her exactly what she needed to restore balance!

I remember thinking that I wish I had that same truth and knowing and here it was, not even 3 days later! Wish granted and fulfilled!!!!! And I get to share it with you!!!!!

The next few pages you will find a ton of tools that will assist your healing, final clearing and resolution! Experiment with them and find out which ones work for you. You'll always have them here for reference. As your healing journey shifts be open to using different healing tools.

Time to Fill Your Tool Kit!

"Listening to Wisdom"

When the body is showing signs of imbalance, be sure to take some time and turn inward.

❖ Create a quiet space so that you can go into a meditative space and have a little chat with your body.

❖ Tune into the imbalance or resistance symptoms and ask the body:

"What am I to learn from this?"

"What resistance have I created or am I holding onto here?"

"Show me what I need to release."

❖ And then wait for the answers – a word, an image, a knowing. Trust what arrives as your truth. You have ALL the answers within you!

❖ As the truth and clarity surfaces, anything that you wish to clear, make a conscious choice to release, clear and reset. Take a deep breath in and release. Continue to release or clear until you feel clear and replenished and neutral.

❖ Then say to your body, "I return to my natural state of being-ness. Perfect health and wellbeing is restored in this moment. All of me resets itself to Source and returns to its perfect rhythm and vitality. I am restored. I am reset. I am perfect, whole and complete!!!

❖ Then from here, you can ignore the symptoms, as they will go away. The body will catch up to the clarity and healing that has just occurred. You can now act as if it's not there or happening because it is complete!

As you vibrationally fine-tune your awareness, you will be able to catch imbalances before they reach the body level. You may become more sensitive and tuned into your emotions or your thoughts and can catch the imbalance at the beginning before it takes root anywhere else.

"Daily Check In"

To enhance your connection and communication to your emotional and mental bodies – Catch it in the act!

Spend time every day, perhaps a few times a day, just checking in to see how you feel.

❖ Notice the quality of your emotions – do you feel peaceful? Uneasy? Emotional? Angry? Happy? Confused?

❖ Whatever is there, notice it and then ask, "What am I .... about?" Use this same line of questioning as before with the body, except ask where the emotions are stirring from and then wait for the answer to percolate into your awareness.

❖ When you have it, repeat the same process as above, clearing and releasing the trigger and make a conscious choice to return to your center or peace or stillness.

❖ Or if you want to simply just practice releasing them, you can do that too! Simply say, "I release and let go. I release and let go. I release and let go. All emotions rinsed clean and clear. I return to my natural state of being. I reset."

❖ And then feel yourself rises back up to that perfect state of stillness or love or peace that you desire.

❖ We don't always have to know what the trigger was. Sometimes we can simply let go, let go, let go and choose differently.

❖ And if you check in and you feel peaceful or happy, then breathe into it and really feel into it. Expand it and let yourself rest in it!

"Checking Your Thoughts"

If you can, every moment be aware of your thoughts. I know this seems impossible or crazy... but just try it out!

❖ Be aware of your thoughts like you were your emotions. What is the quality of your thought? Positive? Negative? Supportive? Destructive? Happy? Sad? Uplifting? Diminishing?

❖ As you become aware of your thoughts, choose to magnify the ones that are supportive and nurturing and uplifting to you. Magnify them until you feel Source energy flowing through you in beautiful strong waves! Let it wash over you!

❖ If your thoughts are not having you feel so good and you feel low energy or diminished, they consciously choose to release them. Breathe them out of your body. Imagine them being swept up by a wave of light, flick them out like flicking dirt away. Do whatever works for YOUR mind to get the clear picture or image of releasing or clearing the thoughts.

❖ Then say to yourself, "I choose thoughts that are supportive and loving and nurturing to my emotions and body. I choose thoughts that are aligned with my higher self or Source. I choose thoughts that heal me!"

❖ Take a deep breath! And then shift your mental focus onto something that creates thoughts that are uplifting...... each of you is different... so choose thoughts that you will enjoy having and that will support your life and connection to self and love of Source energy!

❖ As you shift your thoughts, you allow the channel of energy from Source to flow directly through your crown, into your head, into your mind and your thoughts are instantly uplifted because you feel the experience of Source and clarity and love and truth in that moment! You receive a complete mind, body, spirit download or activation of alignment!!!

❖ And as you feel this and experience it, you will want to think better thoughts because of how they make you feel!!!! Emotionally and Physically!

As we continue to grow and embody the teachings our life will shed certain things and expand upon the new, or what we already knew deep within. We are constantly expanding and contracting in life, just like our breath. And when you feel you're ready for more expansion use your breath… with every inhale feel and think expansion and with every exhale feel and think relaxation, softening, emptying, letting go so that you can allow in the new with each new breath. Your soul is ever moving you in the direction of greater love, greater joy, greater energy. It wants you to have this expanded (love, joy, bliss) experience.

This next section was inspired by a session I had with a loving client who was going through change and spiritual expansion around her body, her relationships and ultimately how she showed up in the world. She suggested that this work was profound and needed to be a part of the book. And so I've transcribed most of our session and gave it some additional form……

Freeing yourself from the mind-trap and effecting positive, powerful change in the world can be the greatest gift to yourself and those around you!

Everything in your world, everything you see, experience, etc. is something that you've ultimately created through your own thoughts – whether you're conscious or unconscious of them. Most of our thoughts are unconscious.

However we can bring more light to our thoughts by focusing our attention there. Imagine the thoughts that you do want to put out there. And then think about the stuff you don't want to put out there. All it is going out into your energy field. The universe is neutral, just like your body, and it receives all signals from your thoughts, higher or lower.

For example: You have the intention or thought to shift how your body is going to look. You sent a signal into your field and something responds. Something arrives in your life like a program for body transformation and you take the steps to get there and your body transforms. The body was neutral all along, it didn't make the choice, you did, from up here (in your mind) and the body responded. That's how ease it can be.

If I think "X", I receive a path that leads to "X", I take the steps that show up and "X" happens.

This is the same with any area of life: your health, how you want your relationships to look and feel, how you want your life to be in general and how you want your finances to look.

It really is simple. It all comes back to choice.

Imagine for a moment that the room you are sitting in is you, not just the physical you that you know and feel... the whole room represents or is you. Out in one corner of the room is your perfect health, in another corner is your perfect relationship, in another area your perfect job, in another area your perfect life, and so on. Everything you've ever wanted exists in this room and space. Somewhere along the way some "stuff" happened that caused pain, doubt, lack, etc. and gave you the opposite to this perfect something. Over time, if we allow this "stuff" to run our life or become our focus, certain beliefs around who or what a person or situation "IS" or what you can expect to see happening gets created. You then continue to live your life from this belief and therefore you see exactly that... it shows up just like that. The lens or filter that you're now seeing the world through, begins to block your full view or ability to anything but the pain or "stuff" and keeps you focus limited to what is right here in front of your filter. You then can no longer see the amazing, perfect life "over there" that you really want.

When we do our spiritual, mindful, self awareness, healing work we begin to remove the limiting filters that have been created and we start to see clearly what we want again. Our eyes and mind open to that perfect version "over there" in the other parts of the room. All of sudden we SEE it! We open up to what was already there... patiently waiting for us to see and receive it! You are now remembering!

HEALING PRACTICE:
Changing YOUR Life

What's the first step to having what you want?

STEP 1. START WITH WHAT YOU DON'T WANT. We see all around us what we don't want in our life. We are so used to seeing what we don't want that we get trapped in the "don't want" and we get more of that because it's where our focus is. The difference here, and how you can free yourself from what you don't want, use it to move you into what YOU DO WANT! Sometimes we have to look at what we don't want to get to what we do want.

Make a list of all the things you don't want:

_____

_____

_____

_____

_____

_____

_____

_____

_____

_____

STEP 2. What YOU WANT? Use the list from above to give you IN-sight as to what you do want. Flip them – use the opposite to what you don't want to get to what you do. Ask yourself, "What do I WANT?" Now your focus shifts to over here. What I want to see is _____. What I want in my life is _____, Saying that you want something is like engaging in it. It is the next step to fully receiving it.

Make a list of all the things you do want:

_____

_____

_____

_____

_____

_____

_____

_____

_____

_____

STEP 3. I CHOOSE. Now we take it up a higher level! We move into the full truth and knowing that what we want, ALREADY EXISTS! That what we want already is, that we want is already there for us. All we have to "do" is step fully into the knowing or reality that it is. And we do this by shifting our focus to: I CHOOSE! For example: I CHOOSE perfect health and well-being. I CHOOSE loving and trusting relationships. I CHOOSE an overflow of abundance and prosperity. Now you're placing yourself on a whole other level of creation and manifestation. By choosing it, you're saying and knowing it is already done and you're just allowing it to come into your life and you're allowing yourself to receive it. You are acknowledging that somewhere inside of yourself it is already done and created and all you're doing is finally choosing it!

Create a list now on what you choose:

_____

_____

_____

_____

_____

_____

_____

_____

_____

_____

We can definitely create from the place of wanting something. However, if you WANT to speed up what you're WANTING in your life, begin to CHOOSE it! That is YOU accepting ALL that you are, all that WANTS to be given to you and you are saying YES in a powerful way to your full life experience! You are saying yes to your creator-universal-god-higher self (more on this later).

_____

Energy influence is a powerful thing.

_____

The coolest thing happens when we do this practice! When we finally choose all the great and good things that we want (even down to the qualities we wish to see in another, for example, "I choose to see my partner as loving, respectful, happy and honouring.")...... you acknowledge the HIGHER version of anything, anyone, or the relationship. You start to see from the eyes of your soul. You are now expanding your energy even more and because we're connected to the world and other people we create an effect all around us that people can feel. Just like when you walk into a room and you're happy but the room feels heavy and all of sudden you feel blah. Or you feel blah and walk into a room that feels happy and light and you feel light and great!

This is energy influence! And we do this all the time... most of the time unconsciously. We are affecting each other all the time through our thoughts and most of the time we are not even aware of it. Consider for a moment how you feel and what you think in any given situation...... have you ever noticed the impact or effects on the people are you? Do people tend to feel uplifted around you? Does the energy stay the same? Do you ever find people finding reasons to get out there faster than expected? What do you think about people in general? What thoughts do you have about the people in your life? Are they loving thoughts, or complaining and judgmental thoughts? Are the thoughts you're sending out helping people or harming people?

It is time that we become more conscious and aware of the thoughts we send out because it does have an effect on the world and the people around us. How would you want to feel? What thoughts would you want others to be having about you? What you want for yourself can be created and given also. Start there and watch how your world and energy level will change. When we have positive thoughts of others, they and we feel uplifted and energized. When we have thoughts that are judgmental and criticizing, they and we feel low energy and sluggish. Remember, you get to CHOOSE your experience with others also by changing and lifting your thinking.

What I think can have an effect on you, and vice versa. That's how powerful we are. When you practice becoming conscious of the thoughts you're sending out, you become a powerful thought projector, chooser and activator for yourself, which expands out and touches every single person you come into contact with! We can either uplift others or put/pull them down... the choice is always yours based on your thoughts.

Helping others by lifting our thoughts and changing our mind about them.

Everyone on this planet is asking for up-lift-ment or evolution... no one really wants to stay in pain even though it seems this way sometimes. From all clients and students I've seen they all have one thing in common – to ease or end suffering (what ever that may be for them). Whenever we reach out for help we asking for release from pain. And so each person will eventually move toward the light… like a moth to the flame. That's why we have so many different healing modalities available to us. It is also why we have so many vices or "outs" or distractions…. We're trying to lift out of pain and discomfort through whatever means possible. And there is a way out you see. It is through your thoughts and your higher mind.

When one person lifts out of the mind-trap he/she creates a field of light so powerful that it "rubs" off on others… energy can affect energy! And when that person feels even a slight lift, their soul recognizes it and wants to go in that direction, and change begins to occur. Also, because you're seeing this person or situation with higher eyes or with higher thoughts (from what you WANT to see), you get to see and experience exactly that because it is where your focus is! HOW COOL!!!! And you also allowed yourself to step out of the illusion or drama of that situation or person's life and move into a more conducive or loving reality.

Now, there may be times and situations when the light and joy within you may trigger a "negative" response in someone else. Lets say you have a person who would be bothered even more by your positivity. This positive energy is simply acting as a trigger for that person to shift. It's like a battle going on within – where one side says stay in drama, don't change and the other is saying it's okay, go to the light. It is often bringing up doubt, insecurity, unworthiness and lack of self acceptance within them. In that moment you have another opportunity to grow and expand. Regardless of what you see you can remain still within and continue to see him/her as love, compassion, acceptance and light.

Another example: Lets say there's someone around you who is "flaring up" and acting inappropriate toward you or is acting like a bull in a china shop. You do not have to stay in the room or stick around watching the destruction happen (unless you want to), or continue to be nice about it. You can lovingly excuse yourself, give yourself a personal "time-out", take care of yourself and reconnect in that moment to your expanded-higher self. When you do this you reset, re-center and realign to a higher truth. Clarity will arise as to how to handle the situation. By not taking it personally, by returning to your higher mind and thoughts, by asking to be shown what to do in this situation you get to expand and so does that person. One of my favourite questions in times like this is, "SHOW ME WHAT TO DO RIGHT NOW." You will receive insight as to how to handle the situation and then you can respond. By practicing this, you will most likely feel a shift within you – feeling more calm, peaceful and more in your heart.

Each situation like this may look different. You may have a different response. There is no one-way of doing things or one response… it's a situation-by-situation basis. If this person is someone you really care for, you may say to him/her, "You know hun, I love you no matter what and I choose you. This is what I want, this is what I choose. I choose this relationship and I want to be in it." Other times you may feel to walk away and not engage. Other times you may need to stand your ground and speak your clarity. Other times you may feel to just be still and quiet and just hug them.

How do I stop seeing the world from judgmental eyes?

Disengage from the world you see out here/there. Sometimes things show up in the world that you would shake your head at and that would feel disturbing. And sometimes it's challenging to look past what you "see". However, you have the sight from your higher eye that will see things very differently than the physical eyes. And that sight will be based on your higher self. As you lift your gaze and say, "Let me know see from a higher perspective. Let me see through higher eyes of light and truth," you will begin to receive IN-sight that will elevate you and completely change your experience or perception of the world around you!

For example: Lets say you're having an argument with someone. You could easily fall into judgment, blame, anger and other lower vibrating emotions and would see pain and wounding. This viewpoint only magnifies and becomes more persistent and frustrating. Instead, choose to lift up out of the drama and ask to see through the eyes of compassion. Continue to keep your focus there and eventually what will happen is your higher self will take over and fill you with love and compassion. That emotional energy will flow out of your field, you will begin perceiving this person in a more loving and accepting way where you can say, "Oh, okay, he/she is just having a flare up. It's not personal. Let me just love him/her anyways," and he/she will feel a shift as well and might even soften as a result. Then the judgment and conflict and ego conversation falls away and becomes non-existent. You rise UP to where you WANT to be and what you WANT to see!

You really can create freedom and healing in any area of your life. It begins with you! It begins with your choice. Start today and choose powerfully what you want, what you want to see, what you want to experience, and what you want to see in the people around you. As you see it all, them all, from a place of light and clarity you will begin to experience exactly that! You have the ability to create either heaven or hell. The choice is yours to make......

Is LIFE happening to me or from me?

Most people experience pain and discomfort in their life because they feel like they don't have control. We have been taught this on so many levels. That power or truth exists somewhere outside of ourselves. That we really don't know anything, that we have to go to others because they know best, that our feelings, intuition or knowing is not true, and that we should give over our power to others because they know more or are more enlightened than us. That when things happen they have nothing to do with us or our creation or thoughts, "It is something that has just happened to me, I'm the victim." We give over our power because we don't want to know that we played a part in the creation of it. We don't want to take responsibility. We have also been taught that "God" or whatever that means is something so far removed, so far outside of us that we have to go somewhere or to someone or to something to connect to "IT". We have forgotten our own POWER – our own creative life force – our own inner god or creator.

And this brings about great fear within us. Fear of the unknown, fear of death, fear of change, fear of power. When we give our power away it's no wonder why so many people feel powerless, anxiety, or out of control and then try to rebalance this by gaining control over something in their life (money, relationship, time, etc.), over-controlling things or people, or extremes of any kind. This all causes constriction, tightness, limitation and fear for losing control so I better hold on tighter. This creates so much stress and exhaustion.

The mind has been allowed to run unconsciously with all sorts of thoughts, many which are not serving us, and this creates a ripple effect down to our emotions, which in turn has our emotions running our life. And then we feel totally out of control. When we experience an imbalance like this we begin the journey of the pendulum swing…… feeling totally in control on one end and then something happens (seemingly out of our control because we forget that we have created this on some level) and we swing to the opposite side and feel completely out of control. And then we try to do something – have power over others, try to control a situation or outcome or have fear rise up that pushes us to take the reins of our life in our hands – and we are once again in control (or so we think ;). Only to begin this cycle or swing all over again. Many people are living their life like this – back and forth – control, fear, lack of control, control. This is the world of duality.

WE do not need to live our life like this. You can lift out of the pendulum game by looking up. Something is holding the top of the pendulum while earth life swings back and forth, and that's where we want our focus to be – UP! You can go up to your higher mind, your higher self, your higher truth and "see" what's really going on in any situation by lifting your gaze. When we do this, truth fills us, clarity rushes in and we realize that we can create our experience by choosing in every moment. We remember that our higher self is working with us and through us... that our thoughts are flowing from us and creating what ever we say YES to.

Creating the Ultimate Relationship of Your Life!

There is a difference between our body, our emotions, our thoughts and our spirit. They are distinct energy bodies that have their own function and purpose. In a balanced, healthy state these systems or energy bodies work together to create perfect harmony, joy, health and beauty, working as one unit. However, for many people there is a disconnection or separation between these aspects, with little understanding of the relationship between them and therefore conflict arises within, each "mind" within each energy body trying to do its thing. It requires our conscious will to choose something different... the willingness to create a new and loving relationship between these four energy systems so that our life can be as we want it to be.

The first step of awareness for most people is of the body – something flares up to get our attention. Remember the body is neutral, awaiting direction from the mind. As we listen and give the body what it needs we harmonize. We often then begin the journey of our emotions... becoming conscious of what we are feeling, what feels good, what doesn't feel good and we tend to gravitate toward a few emotions that we wish to feel most of the time. We then take the journey up to our thoughts... becoming aware of our mind and all that exists there. Becoming aware of thoughts that serve us and thoughts that hurt.

We can easily ease and balance our emotions by refocusing our thoughts. Often when we are having an emotional freak out it's not really what we want to feel. So lets use that and refocus on what I want to feel. And when we do this, we start to feel better. Our emotions do not control our thoughts. Our thoughts dictate our emotions, which translate down and have an effect on our body. Want to change your body, your health, your wealth, your relationships, your experience???? CHANGE YOUR THOUGHTS!

The next stop on our journey of awareness is our spiritual body and truth, where we begin to realize our life has everything to do with us. That we are creating and co-creating with our higher mind-higher self. We begin to remember that we are god… we are it. We are the creators of our experience. The god that we pray to is actually us… our higher, most loving, most expanded self… that only wants the best for us… that loves us unconditionally, that sees the higher version of us and is always holding it for us, waiting for the day that we say yes to it and want to receive it!

If you consider all the spiritual and religious texts, they all say a similar thing: go up and seek god, they speak of ascension, go to the light, resurrection, dying and rebirthing, climbing the ladder to heaven, walking in the valley of darkness so that we can return to the light, focusing on the third eye point to see truth, go within and you shall find truth. They all speak of going up or in… and not going up as in dying or leaving our body or thinking that god is something outside of us… It is for us to look up, or turn within, take our vision up, look up through a higher lens and begin to see truth! Going into the higher mind that IS YOU and that governs your whole life. And then allow it to be a part of life by embodying it.

When you pray to god, you feel better… Why? Because you are connecting to the you that is the higher you… the truth, the all-knowing you and you are taking time to cultivate a relationship with it! You are taking time to acknowledge the higher aspect of who and what you really are! Some people even cry when they experience this because it is so beautiful and profound that it touches our very essence…… we know it to be true and real.

From this perspective, things don't just happen to us. On some level we have agreed to this. We have chosen it – maybe from where and what we don't want, maybe from our fears, maybe from the past, maybe for learning and growth, and hopefully, eventually from our joy, our truth, our wants, our loves.

For example: Lets say you wanted to learn about unconditional love. In order to know unconditional love you need to be able to love no matter what shows us. You would drawn to you experiences or a relationship that would push your buttons and express things that are not loving or may not feel good, or where a person may act mean to you. In that moment you can judge it/them and react to it and keep experiencing situations like this. Or you can get the learning and love them anyways… love them through it all, no matter what shows up. This is loving unconditionally – free from any condition or thing. Love because you love. And once you get the learning… you "graduate" from it and life becomes easy and flowing.

At any moment you can empower yourself and step back into your god-self by accepting responsibility and consciously beginning to choose your thoughts that are in alignment with a higher voice, higher truth, higher mind.

Imagine for a moment your full, most expanded self, your god-self. Imagine all that you could do and create…… You are infinite. You are not limited. You have full creative power. How would your life look? How would your body feel?

From this place of realization… you really DO HAVE A LOT OF SAY in the game of life. You really do have a lot of power in how you want to shape and create it!

As you take this journey of self awareness you begin to establish a relationship within you, between your spirit, thoughts, emotions and body, that can work with you and for you instead of against you. It will be the most valuable relationship you have ever created!!!!

Healing is easy and anyone can do it.

In closing, healing really is simple. It is not this BIG, scary, complicated thing. We all have the ability to heal, to be healed and to be a healer in our own life and in helping others. When we know how to hold space for others we know how to hold space for own stuff when it shows up! Being of service is a wonderful way to grow, expand, extend and give healing and love… and continue our own personal journey of expansion and healing.

Pearce's Healing Story:

I feel this was a great space to share Pearce's journey. He came to me for intuitive healing at the age of nineteen. During the session it was evident that he was way beyond his years in his inner knowing, healing and truth. He carried the energy of shaman – with the ability to heal instantly (self and others). Where had he learned this ability? The answer… within! He had not taken a course on healing, he simply knew it! It was alive and flowing within him and he felt called to learn more about it – to give form to something that was formless at this point. He has grown into a powerful "healer" and facilitator and continues to share his gifts with clients and in his "other work" (conscious-based marketing and graphic design).

Here's what he had to say about his experience: "I've gone to Tara for sessions, completed my Master Reiki training with her and, most recently, finished her course in Advanced Healing. Underlying all the wisdom Tara has to share, what truly helps me expand is her compassion and ability to see me as my highest self. Her dedication to her clients and students allows nothing but growth complete healing on all levels. She doesn't just teach or heal. Tara allows me to feel empowered to use my own skills and apply my own knowledge. She shares the responsibility to heal the world - its people, its time, its space. Life changes when you do."

Pearce Cacalda,
Healer, Artist, Creative

I hope this book has been of service to you, in simplifying the healing process and journey. I hope you begin to see from new eyes......... that there really isn't anything broken in us and that we really are already and always perfect, whole and complete......... we are simply a thought away from remembering that truth in any moment. The instant we remember, we get out of our way, the rush of life force energy can enter once again and we allow the body to realign itself to this higher truth of perfect health and wellbeing!

The circle of life returns us to honouring our experience here in physical form.

In the full clarity and healing and rebalancing, we return full circle to the beginning of the book, where we talk about supporting the being and vessel through food, exercise and root chakra support! Any time during healing or rebalancing, it is important to give the physical body everything it needs to restore the cells to their pristine state. This includes food and nourishment just as much as love and Source energy! Remember, Source energy is in everything! Including being stored in food! So indulge! Let your being receive LOVE and SOURCE ENERGY in every form possible! You will sparkle brighter and brighter every day! Growing more beautiful with every round of the circle, so that your life experience becomes an infinite spiral of light and clarity and love and truth and radiance!

New Healing Habits for the Whole Self:

1. *The body is a communication device or vehicle – always sending us signals of alignment or misalignment. Pay attention to what it's saying and make adjustments accordingly and receive the healing that you require in that moment.*

2. *Healing is a balancing act. There is no one-way to healing. It is not a black-and-white answer or process… but rather a whole lot of grey. Just as we are not linear or two-dimensional neither is healing. It is very much a multi-dimensional phenomenon that requires different tools and methods in any moment. Your "job" is to pay attention, ask the right questions and give what is being asked for.*

3. *Healing is as easy as you think it to be. It can be a quick and easy journey or not. YOU have the power to choose your path, your life, your experience, your thoughts, your emotions and definitely your healing or health and well-being.*

4. *If there's a charge there's something to change.*

FREEDOM

Round and round and round we go
Where it stops nobody knows
Eternal bliss I declare
Ride the spiral and I am there!

Dancing and swirling this world unknown
Together the fabric is delicately woven
Trust I know will guide me there
To insights and wisdom that I shall share.

Fear is gone and choice is present
I choose my life as I am in it
And so it shall be one of love
Of bliss and joy I will become.

More of myself to fully express
I remember this life, there is no test
Only experience and creation abound
Today, I declare that I am found

I set myself free, I am pure Source
And to this truth I step on the course
This game of life I play with ease
I love myself and so I am free.

SPACE FOR YOUR HEALING JOURNEY THOUGHTS

I personally thank you for taking this journey of healing! It takes courage to walk a path of truth and to face yourself......as well as the unknown and your discomforts! I am sooooo grateful for you and proud of every step you've taken!

Every day you have grown! Every day you will continue to grow. Every day you are a new being, fresh in the world! Choose to live and feel and create it the way you WANT it to BE!

Live Vibrantly, Love FULLY and expand JOY-FULLY. I love and appreciate YOU!

Tara xoxoooo

IF YOU WANT MORE – ADDITIONAL SUPPORT FOR YOUR HEALING JOURNEY

Several workshops, classes and courses have been created to assist with your journey of healing and self-awareness. If you are feeling drawn to one-on-one work – healing, energy work, life coaching and mentoring, and Spiritual advising sessions are available. For more information on any of these services or classes, please visit: www.taraantler.com.

One-on-one Intuitive Healing Sessions, Life Visioning and Mentoring. Available globally, in person and by phone/Skype.

Guided Meditation CDs. Tara gently and lovingly guides us through various healing and rebalancing meditations. Available on iTunes – Love Ignites Light Meditation by Tara Antler.

A COURSE IN SELF-HEALING – 8 WEEK PROGRAM

An interactive, practical, playful workshop to bring you into alignment with your perfect health and well-being state. Using the principles and teachings from this book, as well as other tools practiced along the way. Leave feeling balanced, whole, filled with vitality and completely empowered to heal your body, mind and return to highest version of you.

A Course in Advanced Healing – 50 hr program

This course has been designed to go further into the "healing modalities" that have been powerfully practiced by Tara for over twelve years. Taking the best-of-the-best healing practices and delivering them in a way that is in alignment with the ease and flow at which healing actually occurs. For those wanting to further their healing, for self and with others, who want to pursue a career in healing services, for those who facilitate or teach others, and for life coaches or healers who are already on the well-being path.

Living Vibrancy Retreats

Our retreats are created with the great care, compassion and consideration. We choose locations, timing, topics and facilitators based on the theme for each retreat – bringing about massive LOVE, joy, transformation, rest, nourishment, and recalibration. Each retreat offers meditation, yoga, time to play and rest, time to reconnect, energy/body work, natural elements of nature and spiritual insights and teachings. All within a space of complete acceptance so that you feel held and supported.

Reiki Levels 1, 2 and 3 (hours depend on Level)

Reiki or Universal Life Force Energy is a beautifully grounding and expansive healing modality. It is often a foundation for healing. It is unconditional love straight from Source – which can align or heal anything and everything. We simply open our channel of light and allow this amazing energy to flow through!

Living Your Higher Self Series – 6 weeks

An audio/video series that walks you through creating the most important and powerful relationship of your life...to your higher, most expanded self! When you access the higher self, new ways of living and being in the world spring up, allowing your life to be an easy, wonderful and joyful experience!

PRIVATE INNER ALCHEMIST MENTORSHIP - 6 WEEKS

This mentoring program will take into a deeper world within, activating your inner power and your inner alchemist! Discover a new way of living and existing in the world, experience more joy, gratitude and appreciation, enhance all relationships and create an abundant life with a grounded sense of purpose! From this mentoring program you will shift paradigms from "I wish" energy to "I AM" energy and knowing! Become the grand magician of your own wonderful life!

L.O.V.E MENTORING – 6 WEEKS
(LIFE OF VIBRANT EXPRESSION)

This mentoring program will assist you with accessing more of your vibrant self by opening the heart, deepening self-love and allowing your full essence to shine. Your life will completely expand, shift and come to life! You will feel more love, internally and externally, you will feel more connected to your life, and you will wake up every day feeling excited about the life you are living! Every relationship in your life will feel the uplifting effects.

PRIVATE EMPOWERED LIFE DESIGN MENTORSHIP - 8 WEEKS

This mentoring program will take into a deeper world within, activating your inner power to create the life you've always wanted! Discover a new way of living and existing in the world, experience more joy, gratitude and appreciation, enhance all relationships and create an abundant life with a grounded sense of purpose! From this mentoring program you will shift paradigms from "I wish" energy to "I AM" energy and knowing! Become the grand designer of your own wonderful life!

COMPASSIONATE SUPPORT IN YOUR AREA

If you are seeking external support, it is important to go to someone who is highly recommended, referred by someone you trust, or someone who you feel really good about seeing. And give some thought as to what you're looking for, the modality you feel drawn to, and the energetic space that you would like held for you. Each facilitator/healer/practitioner offers a unique healing blueprint – just like a fingerprint. There will be a perfect and natural fit for YOUR PERFECT HEALING!

As a side note: a healing session can be a very deep, personal, vulnerable and opening experience. You want to feel safe, held, loved, supported and well taken care of. This is your time to be nurtured and loved unconditionally. If a practitioner ever judges or reprimands you, you may want to seek out another. Loving and compassionate healing is never judging.

Tara loves supporting the healing work of other practitioners. And so, she has complied a list of some of her favourite "peeps" in the healing industry. They each have a beautiful, loving, powerful and compassionate natural ability to heal and empower. And they have each studied with Tara personally (Living Vibrancy Practitioners™ and/or completed A Course in Advanced Healing™ and/or completed one-on-one Mentoring for Success Program™).

Listed in Alphabetical Order.

Brook Jillian Yantzi – Dancing with Life Facilitator, Youth Leadership Coach, Intuitive Healer, Living Vibrancy Practitioner

Location: Canada; UK; Kenya, Africa; Australia; World-wide.

Email: brookejillianyantzi@gmail.com

Website: www.brookejillian.com

Specialty/Focus: Working with women and youth to love their bodies and themselves, leadership development, anxiety, depression, finding purpose, clarity, ease and passion and help people dance with life.

Ingrid Pulpan – Creative Extraordinaire, Intuitive Healer, Living Vibrancy Practitioner, Reiki Master, Jeweler

Location: Toronto & Burlington, Canada.

Email: ipulpan@gmail.com

Website: coming soon! Please email for more info!

Specialty/Focus: Helps people align to their true being, purpose and self. Each session is designed based on ones needs to eliminate pathogens, emotional traumas, anxiety, depression and spiritual blocks. This in turn helps one to remember their purpose and passion and to live the life that they have always imagined.

King Gabriel Quincy Collymore – Spiritual Healer, Absolute Realization Coach, Reiki Master

Location: Toronto, Barrie & North Bay, Canada; World-wide.

Email: quincycollymore@gmail.com

Website: www.arealizationc.com

Specialty/Focus: Assists others in healing physically mentally and emotionally and demonstrates step by step, how to create the exact lives that they desire. The result is always Perfect Health, Clarity and Fulfillment. Love is Limitless !!!

Morgan Toombs – Healthy Sexuality Counseling, Sexuality Education, Body Image Expert and Coach, Registered Nurse

Location: Toronto, Kitchener & Calgary, Canada; World-wide.

Email: morgan@morganb.com

Website: www.HowToBeSexy.Tv & www.thevibrantyou.ca

Specialty/Focus: Boosting quality of life related to the "softer" sides of sex (body image, esteem, confidence, feelings of power vs powerlessness, relationship, sexual and relational communication and negotiation, life skills related to sex and/or how having a positive self image can dramatically improve their quality of life.

Pearce Cacalda – Intuitive Healer, Living Vibrancy Practitioner, Reiki Master, Artist & Art Director – Spirituality in Marketing

Location: Toronto, Canada.

Email: pearce.cacalda@gmail.com

Website: www.pearcecacalda.com

Specialty/Focus: Helping people of all ages to heal and reconnect with their highest purpose and creative power.

Robin A Lind – Retreat Facilitator (Hawaii & Australia), Healer, Living Vibrancy Practitioner, Artist, Designer, World Traveller

Location: Ontario, Canada; Hawaii, USA; Australia.

Email: info@robinsretreats.com or robin@robinsretreats.com

Website: www.robinsretreats.com

Specialty/Focus: Robin's reassuring, loving, joyful, and supportive manner help people re-connect to their true voice and inner being. She works with colour, art, crystals and healing energy in a one-on-one setting, as well as group and retreats.

WE WOULD LOVE TO BRING HEALING TO YOU, YOUR EVENT, LOCATION OR ESTABLISHMENT!

To order additional books or to buy in bulk, please contact The The Academy of LIGHT at 647-991-9366.

Or go to www.Amazon.ca or www.Amazon.com to purchase individual or multiple copies. It/they will be mailed to you directly from Amazon.

If you are interested in or wish to have this book at/in your establishment please contact us at 647-991-9366 or info@taraantler.com .

To request author information, or to have Tara speak at your event or host a "Heal Your Life" book event/workshop, or for other media requests, please contact Media Relations at 647-991-9366 or info@taraantler.com .

Made in the USA
Charleston, SC
06 November 2014